PRAISE FOR *YOU ARE M*

"Thank you for teaching us how to love our neighbors."

The Sander Family, Ben, Nancy, Belle, and Aidan

"Loving one's neighbor is a central tenet to the Christian Faith. That love is more than a word or a kind gesture; it often requires meeting people where they are and ministering to them in the challenging and even ugly aspects of life on the street or in a shelter. The reflections in this book come from a woman who puts herself out there in order to get to know her brothers and sisters in real ways. This is what our Lord meant when he said, 'Do this in memory of me.'"

Most Rev. William A. Wack CSC, Bishop
Diocese of Pensacola-Tallahassee, Florida

"From the beginning of Judy Knotts' published newspaper articles, my 90-plus-year-old mother and I became overwhelmingly inspired by this honest and courageous woman who dared to share such candid and heart-breaking stories of our homeless friends in Austin. We felt as if we were taking every fearful step of her journey with her, and as Judy Knotts shows us in her book, forcing ourselves to recognize that homelessness is not only them, but all of us—our families, friends, neighbors, and even fellow church members. In whatever way God shows us our path, I hope you and I will be guided through this book journey with the following verse from Joshua Chapter 1:9, *'Have I not commanded you? Be strong and courageous. Do not be terrified; do not be discouraged, for the Lord your God will be with you wherever you go.'*"

Ruth Brown (and Jacqueline Richardson)

"A cardboard mattress; a concrete box spring; perhaps a newspaper pillow. These are the 'comforts of home' that homeless men and women lie down to each and every night. It is easy to ask, 'Why would God allow such suffering in the world?' or 'Is there any hope for these people?' It is much more difficult to immerse yourself in who these men and women are as Jesus knows them—by name and by story. Melding grace with a fiery passion for serving the poor, Dr. Judy Knotts eloquently captures first-hand the realities of life, death, and Salvation through Christ's love in the streets of Austin, Texas, in *You Are My Brother*."

Brody Roush, friend and mentee of Dr. Judy Knotts

"Dr. Knotts eloquently shows us the reality of the human experience. We are all connected as brothers and sisters through a unity that was beautifully crafted by God, so that we could share and find meaning in each other's successes and failures; talents and flaws; and joy and struggles."

Daniel Luque, former high school student of Dr. Judy Knotts

"Thanks for writing the articles in the Statesman. I read them while I was in prison and it helped me."

Billy, former inmate

"Whenever I read Judy Knotts' stories of connection with folks who live on the streets of Austin, I'm jealous. I want so much to be like Judy. How in the world does she do it? I think her formula is very simple. While you and I see someone to avoid, Judy sees a human being created by God for love and companionship. Through her writings, she teaches us how to be with people who are very different from us but who share our common humanity. In our time, this may be the very best gift of all."

Rev. John Elford, Senior Pastor
University United Methodist Church, Austin, Texas

"Great cities of the United States are awesome reflections of the unfolding human story of the 20th and 21st centuries. All of our cities are centers of art and culture and are productive beyond anything that our past generations could have dreamed. Despite the material blessings, without exception, our cities are encircled by a sizeable number of neighborhoods marked by agonizing poverty, failed schools, disease and crime. Together we have the resources and know-how to remove the blight of our cities!

"We lack the know-how to act because most of us do not see and do not feel the pain and suffering in the lives of our neighbors. Our freeways have been designed to whisk us from the economic center of the cities to comfortable suburban neighborhoods.

"Dr. Judy Knotts has provided us with the insight to this silent issue with an excellent book entitled *You Are My Brother*. Dr. Knotts left her academic environment often and went to the back streets and alleys visiting homeless people in their world. She did not just get to know them, she became a knowing, loving friend. Anyone reading *You Are My Brother* will see and feel more clearly the suffering beyond those freeway walls and hopefully consider in the never ending struggle for a more just and loving society."

Most Rev. John E. McCarthy
the late Bishop Emeritus Diocese of Austin, Texas

"Simply, Judy Knotts is one of my heroes! She is able to dive deep into the grittiness of who we are as humans and find those gold veins of goodness that are part of all humans."

Alan Graham, President, Mobile Loaves & Fishes

"Every day I read three new sources: the *Austin American-Statesman,* the *New York Times* and the Bible. All of these sources are filled with stories of lies, partisanship, quarreling and violence—including the Bible.

"Today the Good News was not from the Bible, but from Judy Knotts, a frequent contributor; I have several of her columns I have clipped and saved for years.

"Her example of the unconditional love of a dog for his person as proof of God's unconditional love for each one of us made my day. Judy's theology is spot-on, as is her compassion for her fellow creatures, human and canine. Thank you for giving your readers another reason to look forward to the Saturday Statesman."

Bonnie Boorman, Georgetown, Texas
From a letter to the editor of *Austin American-Statesman*

YOU ARE MY BROTHER

LESSONS LEARNED EMBRACING A HOMELESS COMMUNITY

JUDITH D. KNOTTS

NEW TRIPOLI PRESS
Austin, Texas

YOU ARE MY BROTHER

LESSONS LEARNED EMBRACING A HOMELESS COMMUNITY

By Judith D. Knotts

Published by
New Tripoli Press
Austin, Texas

Cover Design and Interior Layout and Design | Yvonne Parks | PearCreative.ca
Proofreader: Clarisa Marcee | AvenueCMedia.com
Index | Elena Gwynn | quillandinkindexing.com
Photograph of Laura Tanier © Michael O'Brien. All rights reserved.

Library of Congress Control Number: 2018905638
ISBN (print): 978-1-7322820-0-1
ISBN (Kindle): 978-1-7322820-1-8
ISBN (ePub): 978-1-7322820-2-5

DEDICATION
FOR STREET FRIENDS

* deceased

JP	Chris	Bruce
Vernon	Fred	Mark
Wolf	Jeff and Jeff*	Boston Chris
Tony	Bridget	Joe
Carnival Man	Charles	James
Christopher	Jim	Lloyd
Laurie	Judith	Larry
Moses	Kristen	Kurt
Judy Lynn	Mighty Mouse	Eddie
Ronald	Laura*	Jerry
Frederick	Mark	Nathan
Cross Maker	Beth*	Angie
Ellis	Sam*	Brian
Paul	Steve	Dawn
Rail Hopper	David	Bubba
Charlie	Avon	Dwayne
Sheila	Chief	Anastacia
Dawn	Darrell	Shelly
Venice	Rodeo	Zach
Eddie	Preston	Teresa
Angie	John	The 3 Steves
Jerry	Popcorn	Victor
Kim	Little Feet	Shannon
The Twins	Bear	Gabriel
Hal	Shorty	Debbie
Jose	Reptile	Josh
Carl	Momma	Lucille
Richard	Mississippi	Mark
Michael	Crash	Ricardo
Lawrence	William	Michael
Sam	Freddie*	Carmen
Sheila	Tyrone	Emily

Our chief want is someone who will inspire us
to be what we know we could be.

—RALPH WALDO EMERSON

TABLE OF CONTENTS

FOREWORD

Judy Knotts sees people. Not just the way you and I might see people. She sees deep into their souls, into their hearts. She sees them as unique individuals as well as for their recognizable humanness.

This collection of essays, most of which have been published within the last two decades in the faith column of the Austin American-Statesman, gives insight into the treasure that is Judy Knotts.

It also invites you to find the Judy Knotts in you.

Knotts offers a lesson in treating everyone with dignity; a lesson in meeting people where they are; a lesson in putting away all the judgmental thoughts we have about fellow humans, and encourages us to open our hearts and our minds to everyone.

Readers of the Statesman have responded in thoughtful ways to the words of Judy. No other faith columnist has elicited as many emails of praise to her editors. Readers always comment about what a good person Judy is, how she challenged them to look at another person in a different way, how they were going to roll up their sleeves and act.

Quite frankly, Judy shakes us out of our complacency in loving ways and invites us to act. It's not enough to hand a homeless person a dollar or a package of food or a bottle of water. What everyone craves is compassion, understanding and dignity. How can we be the bearers of those things? How can we look into another person's eyes and really see them for who they are, not what we think they are?

I invite you to take each essay into your heart. They will change you, make you a better person, make you see people differently, make you see the world differently. Sometimes she will make you angry that anyone suffers and that no one has solved the problem of homelessness. Sometimes she will make you weep at the story you have just read.

Take your time with these essays. Drink them in and savor them.

It has been my pleasure to get to know Judy as a person and as a writer as her editor at the Statesman for the past six years.

Her words have changed me, I know her words will change you, too.

Nicole Villalpando
Specialty Editor, Austin American-Statesman

PREFACE

We are a story people on the planet. From creation tales, to Greek and Latin myths, to the Bible, to narratives today on screen, we engage, we listen. And we read—to learn, to be entertained, to be reassured, and to understand who we are. *You Are My Brother* is a collection of thirty-three short stories, all true, with a thread connecting them. They are about my encounters with homeless people and the epiphanies that we both experienced from meeting.

Since 2008, I have been a regular contributor to the *Austin American-Statesman* and most of the stories in this book have appeared there. Because of this consistent inclusion and popularity, I have come to believe that we all want stories that may be unfamiliar to us in context, but contain real characters that we might never have had the chance to meet. In these stories, the goodness I discover and share changes readers' perception of homeless people and of us.

In many selections, despite the often uplifting messages of brotherhood and hope, I do not shy away from the harshness of the homeless life and where truth is required mention guns, robbery, drugs, dirt, bed bugs, death, as well as illness of body and mind. All of this and more, is contrasted with spirituality and amazing kindness. The dichotomy is what keeps me among homeless people and grabs the readers' attention again and again.

The world today is full of tragedy—violence, wars, bombings, shootings, hunger, and, of course, homelessness, which is an international, national, and local threat and problem. The population of the homeless community is growing and solutions are being sought, but are scarce. Men and women, teens and seniors, people just like you and me want some sort of illumination to lessen the pain. People of all ages long for good news, no matter how small or insignificant it may seem. The big problems of the world are daunting and we cannot even wrap our arms around the issues; however, little stories of individuals can make us believe that each small step matters and that we can all play a part in making our world a better place.

The structure of the book, in addition to the stories themselves, is what gives *You Are My Brother* its distinctive quality. These short takes are for people who may have limited time or do not have interest in a lengthy text, yet long for a story that captures their hearts. You may decide to read through, beginning to end. If you are impatient as I often am to get the flavor of a book, you may want to go chapter by chapter or skim the titles to see what grabs your attention. It may be helpful to note that each one of these stories stood alone in the newspaper, so readers had the time to read and then reflect upon what they read—the essence of finding meaning.

Many times readers, some of whom I know and others who are strangers, refer to a story by its title or topic and tell me, "I loved *Wanting the Whole Pie*, it made me smile." "The story about *Freddie*, made me cry." "The story about *The Good Thief* opened my eyes and removed some of my prejudice, thank you." Local clergy and ministers from other states have written to me that they used one of my stories in their weekly sermon or articles, which makes me want to keep writing. Some resourceful readers have tracked me down after reading an article and brought me hand-crocheted blankets to take to the homeless shelters or have given me money to buy underwear and socks for those without. Readers have been touched by the stories and have responded with generosity and sometimes personal sacrifice.

Many of these stories have been written with Austin in mind since that is where I live; however, homelessness and our response as individuals or a community is the same everywhere—in a small town or a big city. What do we see? What do we do?

INTRODUCTION

In the spring of 2003, within 72 hours, my stunted view of the world changed. Before that it seemed forever I went through life like a harnessed mule wearing blinders, rarely veering left or right, just mindlessly pulling the plow behind me, home to work to grocery to church.

Alan Graham, founder and CEO of Mobile Loaves & Fishes, announced the first "Street Retreat" in Austin and I scoffed. Who in their right mind would leave the comfort and safety of their home and voluntarily take to the streets? I tried to talk a business associate out of going. Then, I had the strangest experience, almost immediately; I decided to go as well, despite my words of warning to him.

As potential participants, we gathered for weeks to pray and get a sense of the journey. I began to understand what this was all about. It was not a field trip to learn about homeless people. It was a catalyst for growth and a chance to get closer to God. And so it began. We were dropped off downtown with empty pockets—no money, no credit cards, and no cell phones. For 72 hours we stood in line for food, slept when and where we could, and searched for welcoming rest rooms.

On the streets, I was disoriented and felt I had been dropped in a strange land. Traveling by foot for everything was a new way of life for me. Landmarks were not tall buildings I knew or familiar restaurants, but benches or walls to perch upon and garages and overhangs to find refuge from storms. Without a car, the steep hills of Austin surprised me and I searched for flat terrain. Sleeping in fits and starts, in strange places with strange noises of the city, left me fatigued by the second day. Eating one meal a day, made me sluggish.

My concentration was on life's basics—where to eat, where to sleep, where to urinate and defecate, and how to cope with Mother Nature's whims of heat, or cold, or rain. By the end of day one, I looked homeless and began to feel like an outcast. People, the kind that I would have formerly associated with, the *suits* with jobs, dissed me. They rarely gave me eye contact, a smile, or a word, and often went out of their way to avoid me. I began to grasp discrimination in my gut.

Because of this experience, the blinders are off and I now see homeless people everywhere and begin to understand the nuances a bit. For the homeless population, a pecking order exists like it does for the rest of society. At the top are those people who have part-time minimum wage work or a social security check that may allow them to live in a housing project, a trailer park or a rooming house, at least for a time. On the next rung down, are those who might have a temporary slot in a shelter, or they might sleep in a car, a tent, or briefly on someone's sofa.

The bottom tier hides in alleys. Sometimes just a single person is visible sleeping under newspapers or sitting next to a stuffed shopping cart. In certain alleys in our city; however, I have discovered that small communities exist in squalor. Here, people hang out at different times of the day with nothing to do and no place to go.

After my first immersion of 72 hours living on the streets, I continued to explore the world of the homeless community whenever I could. Driving cautiously one evening, I threaded my car through a narrow alley and the bleakness overwhelmed me. Soiled clothes were heaped in piles. Trash was underfoot, caught on tree branches, and plastered against walls and fences. From an overturned oil drum, liquor was poured for those who were interested. Drug swaps were more secretive. Residents sat on rotted timbers or plastic milk crates. Twosomes propped each other up and singles leaned against a chicken wire fence. Strangely, there were as many women here as men, and age seemed not to matter at all. By any gauge of common sense, this should have been a dangerous area, yet it felt sort of familial. Smiles surfaced on a few faces, especially when they noticed that food was being offered. A lone person asked only for a hug.

At first glance, this alley seemed incredible and practical questions popped up. Where did these folks sleep amid the pot-holes and broken glass? How did they find food? Where did they empty their bladders and bowels, and where did they bathe? What did they do when it stormed or soared to triple digits?

Much later, deeper questions floated to the surface of my brain. Why were they hidden? Why did so few people see them? Where were the police officers and social workers? Friends, who at one time were homeless and lived in this kind of hell-hole and worked their way up the ladder to health, sobriety, and a kind of stability, acknowledged to me that they once had been part of this alley life, which I never knew existed.

So what should we do with the alley people? Is "do" even the right approach, the right verb? Or is this a poignant example of the age-old battle between individual freedom and society, a sort of balancing act with privacy teetering on one end of the see-saw and propriety ensconced on the other? Should we help those who might not want to be helped? Whose job is it to care? Putting all my philosophizing aside, isn't the real question, who will show them that they are loved?

Memorandum to self: "In the evening of our lives, we will be judged on love alone." (St. John of the Cross)

Okay, how, I wonder, do I love these people? How do I keep my heart open? And why do I do it? Why do I find myself drawn to the streets every so often to keep this homeless wound open? It might be 24 to 72 hours spent living with homeless people. Or it might be a night sleeping with homeless men in an emergency shelter when it freezes. Most other folks can stay focused on homelessness by reading articles or watching documentaries and be moved to compassion. I too process these words and film clips, but for me it is so easy to swallow them and go about my life of comfort undisturbed enough to act. High-thread-count sheets and fluffy towels conveniently wrap a cocoon around my life. It takes a periodic dose of reality to shake me into sanity, into salvation.

So I go out again to be among the homeless folks. On the streets, penniless, everything grabs my attention. I see Brad, the courtly gentleman absentmindedly wandering in the park, conversing with himself. I notice the sparrow-like old woman sleeping in an alley while people step over her. At dusk, I search for a place to sleep in a secluded parking lot or doorway and in this setting sense the anxiety swirling around Brenda who is cutting her arms to relieve some unnamed pain. I hold hands in evening prayer with homeless friends, and marvel as they give thanks for another day lived, and then catch Samuel's toothless smile tossed to me as I try to burrow deep in my blanket. I hear Hector coughing throughout the night without complaint and experience the full bladder feeling at dawn when walking the streets looking for a rest room. I feel bone-tired after spending a night on concrete made bearable by a piece of cardboard and wait in line for food graciously served by church people.

Why does it matter—cultivating an open wound? In these intimate, intense immersions, I am reminded that homelessness is not only them, but us, all of us, our families, our friends, and our neighbors. It is not just the *fliers* on busy street corners with their signs asking for money, the drug and alcohol addicts hanging out on street corners, or the physically and mentally challenged in line at the soup kitchens. It is not the thousands of nameless homeless people living on the streets, in the woods, in cars, in tents, in sheds, in abandoned buildings, on rooftops, and under bridges or finding one night stands in shelters and cheap motels. It is Brad the wanderer and the sleeping sparrow-woman. It is Hector who coughs, Brenda who cuts, and Samuel who smiles.

Keeping the wound open helps me look homeless people in the eye and warmly recognize their presence as my brother and sister.

Cardiac prognosis: no miraculous healing, merely intermittent pain inching me toward communion.

BROTHERHOOD

We need each other desperately to function, to live
a dignified life full of meaning and gratitude.

YOU ARE MY BROTHER, AREN'T YOU?

The title for this book is inspired by a real-life incident, and fact is often more gripping than fiction. One evening in the spring of 2008, I headed downtown to share a bounty of donated food that was stashed in the back of my truck. Stacked in large containers were all of the "fixings" for first-class fajitas—cilantro-seasoned rice, charro beans, pico de gallo, grilled beef and chicken, shredded cheese, sour cream, guacamole, and tortillas. As standard procedure, I always have paper plates, napkins, and serving utensils on hand to facilitate any spontaneous gift of food.

Since it was getting dark and my truck was beginning to smell like a Mexican take-out, I skipped the solo street inhabitants and small groups in the parks, bus stops, and street corners and headed to where I knew a large number of homeless people would be gathered at the Salvation Army, (the Sally) and the Austin Resource Center for the Homeless, (the ARCH). At any time of day, but particularly at night this location can sizzle with pent-up frustrations. Empty pockets and empty stomachs, the urge for drugs, alcohol or sex, the disappointment of not getting into one of the shelters, the longing for trustworthy relationships, and endless fatigue can stir up emotions often ending in shouting matches or worse.

Pulling up to the curb between the two buildings, I got out, popped the back of my truck open and said to the folks present, "Come get in line, I have really good food for you tonight!" Eager to eat, they mostly complied with my request for order with only a minimum of pushing and shoving. Since I promised to make each fajita to order, I asked for their patience. This worked pretty well until one man, angry to the core at some un-named demon, came up to the front of the line and yelled in my face, "Who are you? And why are you here?" Without missing a beat, I said, "You are my brother, aren't you?" This sudden response startled all of us. Wherever that idea came from will forever remain a joyful mystery, but I was grateful for the gift of words that tripped so easily off my tongue. Hearing this simple statement had a profound effect upon my accuser. He literally stopped in his tracks, physically and emotionally deflated like someone had just pricked his angry bubble with a pin. He then hung his head, whispered, "Yes" and got in line.

The crowd breathed a collective sigh of relief that peace was restored and we got about our business of serving and being served. Sometime later as the emotional roller coaster settled down, another man in the crowd said, "Say where did all of this great food come from?" I answered, "A retirement party." He kept questioning, "Whose retirement?" When I said, "Mine," he and his buddies were shocked and said, "You mean to tell us that you came here, to us with your party food?" I replied, "Yes."

Suddenly the fajita making and munching took on a whole new significance to them. They felt invited to a party, perhaps a little late, but still invited. The celebratory event fired their enthusiasm and captured their imagination. They wanted to know what my job was, and hooted with laughter when I told them that I was head of a school. Many in the line assured me that they had spent their share of time in the principal's office, which was not hard to believe. Once they got into the groove of a retirement party, they wanted to know my plans for the future. I told them the truth, I had no plans. So they set to work designing my new life. After some creative solutions and high-spirited debates, they decided that I was just "to kick back and watch Oprah every day."

Smiling, I realized neither friends nor colleagues had treated me so tenderly in suggesting retirement activities. The night ended full circle giving and receiving, receiving and giving, the heart of brotherhood beating soundly.

SOLIDARITY

"But familiarity breeds compassion and even affection. Quite simply, living side by side, you can't pretend they're not there," states Sarah Turnbull, a young Australian woman who immigrated to France.

She is referring to the clochards in Paris, who due to medical, financial or familial circumstances live on the streets. According to Turnbull's book *Almost French*, clochard means "tramp." She wrote, "The word originated at the old Les Halles market where a bell or cloche used to toll at the end of every day when it was time to close the stalls. It became tradition that when the ringing had stopped, any leftovers and overripe produce were given to the homeless and the hungry."

With the famous market gone, soup kitchens, churches, neighborhoods and individuals have tried to fill the void and feed the homeless in this city of exquisite beauty and world-renowned cuisine.

When visiting Paris, I saw the same faces of poverty that I see in Austin. They don't assault you, but if you look carefully in doorways in the early morning, or under bridges at night, they are there with their meager belongings often serving as pillows. And we too in Austin try to take care of our own hungry brothers and sisters at Caritas, Angel House, First United Methodist Church, or University United Methodist Church, and by the daily truck runs of Mobile Loaves & Fishes.

Turnbull writes, "I'd never been drawn to any kind of charity work in Australia. But then I'd never seen people sleeping on cold concrete outside my apartment before either; never lived in a place where homeless people were so woven into community life. Sometimes it's unsettling, privilege and poverty so closely mixed. The disparity is sharpest in winter, when each year several clochards die of cold in Paris. Meanwhile, the shops along Rue Montorgueil fill with the traditional pre-Christmas luxuries." We are no different. They die on our streets while we drown ourselves in holiday madness.

On Thanksgiving Day, I drive through the nearly deserted streets of downtown Austin looking for homeless folks who might enjoy a familial favorite—generous slices of roast turkey, homemade stuffing and cranberry sauce artfully balanced between two pieces of bread. I find them wandering alone, mostly, blocks or steps away from some of our fanciest restaurants and shops where holiday lights flicker in every window.

A few years ago I set out with my annual deliveries, and being an efficient sort, I estimated my personal turkey run should take about an hour. No big deal; I was delighted that the end of this Thanksgiving outreach was in sight and eagerly looked forward to enjoying my own fat turkey sandwich at home. God, as usual, had other plans.

By 4:30 I finished delivering all of the Thanksgiving bags, tiptoeing past several gentlemen who were dozing in the afternoon sun, and I was ready to head home. Suddenly an old friend from the streets flagged me down. I stopped, and we sat on a park bench to catch up. Soon others joined us. We laughed, told family stories and reminded each other how important it is to have friends who care for us.

As we visited, the sun began to set, the air grew chillier and the bench got harder. The grackles swarmed overhead and even left a reminder of their presence on my sweatshirt, which my homeless friends noticed and enjoyed. Just for a moment, I was one of them and at the mercy of the great outdoors.

Surprisingly, as I said goodbye to my homeless friends in the rapidly approaching darkness, the homemade turkey sandwiches faded into the background, upstaged by heartfelt solidarity. Turnbull was right, familiarity does breed compassion, and even affection.

As we enter the season of Advent, a time of joy and anticipation for Christmas, where gift-giving is often expected and routine, I hope I can recall the lesson these homeless people taught me. The gift of self, the gift of time, the gift of connecting is all that matters.

The tangible gift, if there is one indeed, should be a mere symbol of our love for each other. But I should have known this; Christ's coming was the ultimate gift of self, showing us the way.

HOSPITALITY

Early one morning, I left the parking lot where I had slept with homeless folks and walked toward the center of town to get a ride home. Along the way, I passed two men on a bench. I think they were surprised to see me bundled in a fleece jacket, toting my backpack and blanket. I stopped and we visited. Tyrone was a beautiful blue-black man who once had been a heavyweight boxer. His bench companion was Rodeo, a scrawny bearded white man who once had been a fiddler in rodeos. When Tyrone discovered that I was originally from Pennsylvania as he was, we became fast friends discussing features of our native state.

At some point, Tyrone said, "Do you drink?" I answered, "Yes, but not to excess." He jumped on my strange remark saying, "Well, I do!" Then his ham-sized hand reached into a pocket, pulled out a half-pint bottle and offered it to me. This was a first and I was surprisingly honored; however, declined a drink—perhaps the hour or just imagining my lips on that bottle made me pass on this kind offer.

Several blocks closer to downtown, I smiled seeing the water fountain in front of St. Austin Catholic Church. It was put there by Father Chuck who realized, "the street youth were finding it harder and harder to find water...."

As for hospitality in the food world, no one in my estimation topped Lola, The Nubian Queen who operated a Cajun restaurant in the Rosewood section of Austin. Her soul-filled food and spirit were a staple in this neighborhood that reached out to you with huge colorful graphics on the walls of her restaurant—a striking African-American woman and an alligator wearing a chef's hat.

Lola's free Thanksgiving feasts were legendary for those in the know and in need. From her cramped kitchen she produced the best turkey I have ever tasted as well as candied yams, macaroni and cheese, cornbread stuffing, and green beans. I treasured being her waitress. Before the meal was served, Lola came outside and smiled—her gold front tooth and gold high-top sneakers flashing in the sun—then gathered us hand-in-hand for a communal prayer of thanksgiving. Sadly, her restaurant has closed.

An extraordinary example of hospitality that I am aware of happened during WWII. My friend Joost who was 6 at the time and his brother who was 1, were taken in by a Dutch Catholic family who had children of their own. Joost's parents who knew the Germans were rounding up Jews and taking them away, wanted to save their children, so they gave their baby and their young son to a Catholic family in a desperate act of love. In another act of love, the Catholic father said to Joost, when he arrived, "You must do everything we do as a family so you will not be caught by the Nazis, but you do not have to believe."

Tyrone, Father Chuck, Queen Lola, and the Dutch Catholic dad, all hospitality heroes, each in a unique way, offered drink, food, and shelter—no questions asked—showing us how it's done.

So what are we to do? Small steps might be the answer. Maybe help an evacuee or a refugee who is overwhelmed. Maybe buy a drink for a stranger in the coffee shop. Maybe teach a child to invite all newcomers to sit at the lunch table. Or maybe hand a homemade turkey sandwich to someone flying a sign, "hungry" on Friday after Thanksgiving. Hospitality at its best is a person-to-person thing.

Before hotels wanted us to believe that hospitality was their idea, hospitality was customary in many cultures and always biblical. In Genesis 18 and 19, Abraham and Lot extended a welcome to strangers—water to bathe their feet, food, and a place to rest. Jesus, in his public ministry, depended upon the kindness of strangers for food, drink, and lodging.

Biblical persuasion: "Do not neglect to show hospitality to strangers for by this some have entertained angels without knowing it." Hebrews 13:2—this is the **what**. "Let all that you do be done in love." 1 Corinthians 16:14—this is the **how**.

Life's choices.

WANTING THE WHOLE PIE

Imagine a super-sized sixteen dollar pie with distinct quadrants of different summer fruits all topped off with a designer lattice crust. This sat in a peek-a-boo box on a food truck, the only beauty queen on the stage surrounded by wannabe contestants in zip lock bags… day-old scones and store-bought vanilla wafers. The pie's star quality radiated.

As homeless men and women lined up beside the food truck where I was handing out dinner bags of sandwiches, fruit, and dessert, most looked at the box and said nothing. It must have looked out of place to them. But mid-way through serving, a disgruntled man strode up and said, "Gimme that there pie."

There is no real training for managing this kind of behavior. You just kind of go with your gut, but being a school principal helps. In every school, there are some students, and sadly some parents, who demand the red crayon, the front seat on the bus, or a favorite teacher. Believing we are all capable of change, I always felt that part of my job was re-aligning attitudes, selfish to selfless.

So I asked the pie lover, to look at the line behind him that stretched out for a half block or more, which he did. Then I said, "How can I give you the whole pie and ignore those folks behind you in line?" He stopped for a moment and thought, perhaps for the first time about his wants, and the needs of his fellow street people in line. As I hoped, he got it and simply said, "Okay." Then I promised that if everyone got food, we would figure out a way to cut the pie in slices and hand them out, encouraging him to stick around.

With no serving utensils, plates or silverware on the truck, we managed to be creative and used the back of a new comb (that had been sealed in plastic) for a knife. With great care, we lifted the pieces and in lieu of plates, placed them on top of plastic bags. Surprisingly, we thought to ask what fruit they favored. We were all delighted with the outcome, even the outspoken man who wanted the whole pie, but got a piece instead. What I saw on his face while he munched on his pie was pride and a newly polished self-confidence. He knew he had done the right thing and it felt good.

Don't we all secretly want the whole pie at times, but find ourselves too embarrassed to admit this to family, colleagues, and friends? Or maybe we do speak up, push to the front of the line and say in our own way, "Gimme that!" The pie may be a pie, or it may be the highest salary, the biggest house, the most sought after gadget, or the most powerful position.

What in the world gets us out of this self-centered way of living? It may be parents who are smart enough to instill values of justice. It may be grandparents who model restraint. It may be teachers who expect a class to cooperate. It may be strangers who stop to be kind and shock us with a generosity of spirit. It may be a church or temple where music and prayers and rituals focus on love of God and neighbor. Other things such as scouting and service projects might shore up the ethic of care that helps us become compassionate human beings.

And yet we're always tempted. Wanting the whole pie lurks in the shadows of our lives. With a little prompting from each other, I wonder…can we pause long enough like the desperate man in line who said, "Gimme that there pie" and consider what other routes are possible to become our best selves? We desperately need to help each other slew, or at least tame this selfish dragon living inside each one of us.

In many faith traditions, we are our brother's keeper. This complex and challenging philosophy encompasses a whole lot of things, but I suspect, on a very practical level, a good place to start is simply by reminding one another to share a piece of the pie.

THE UMBRELLA

"You remembered" he said shyly, and then a slow smile began to light up his face as if a carol, "Peace on earth, Good will toward men" were being sung to him alone. It was a small miracle that he even saw the umbrella nearly hidden under the boxes and bags in the back of my truck.

I had decided to collect the leftovers from Christmas parties on the last day of school and go to the streets to share with those who had no parties. For years I had done this alone, but this time, two colleagues, Coach Kunz and Coach Silva asked if they could join me. Praise God! It was not a job for one person! Feverishly we re-organized containers of cheese, fruits, snacks, and candies into individual Ziploc bags. Cookies baked with love and tucked into Christmas packages by three spirit-filled women who manage the school cafeteria set a standard we could not meet; however, we did our best. The overall bounty filled the back of my SUV to the brim.

My friend, Moses who wished for an umbrella was our second stop. He lives in an alley about a half block from a busy intersection in East Austin. When we pulled into his spot, there he stood sock-footed, cotton in his ears to block the wind, layers of clothing swaddling him, and a lady's crocheted hat on his head. He was a joyous sight! Behind him was a wheel chair from an earlier time when his legs didn't work well. Now it is his parlor chair or closet depending upon need. Dumpster cardboard nearby becomes his camouflaged bed each night. Looking at this modest collection of things, I asked if he would like a tarp I had in the truck, since wet weather is a scourge of homeless living. He replied, "No thanks, I have one, give that to someone else."

Moses was truly pleased with the recycled giant golf umbrella that would provide a roof over his home, so we moved on. As I backed out of the alley and looked in the rear-view mirror, I saw tears rolling down Coach Silva's face. "Are you all right?" I asked. This burly former professional soccer player said, "We have so much. He has so little, yet he is teaching us to share!" And then I wondered, from years of doing this sort of thing alone, had I become immune to the lessons learned on the streets? Maybe fresh eyes needed to remind me.

On our next two stops we handed out food packages to nearly 100 people. Toward the end we were merely handing out pretzels to open hands. We apologized for the little we had left, but folks were grateful none the less.

As we headed home, we noticed a man alone in the far corner of a loading dock. His back was to us and his trousers were drifting down to his knees. It was hard to tell if he were relieving himself or shooting up. Coach Silva and I got out of the car, waited a bit, and then walked slowly toward him. He seemed surprised that we were there and staggered to meet us. All the while this young reed-thin man struggled to pull up his pants that seemed too large and tugged at the belt in vain.

When we came face to face, his pain engulfed us. His eyes were glazed, his nose ran, and he drooled like a teething baby. I reached out to him and offered what we had left, an apple and an orange. He took one in each hand, stuffed them in his pockets and continued to fumble with the belt. I hesitated for a minute wondering… should I help him hitch up his pants and fasten the belt? Perhaps wisely I decided no, it would strip him of any dignity. He turned away and we did as well, all of us hurting.

Hunger is real in Austin, but it is the one-to-one connection and caring that homeless people really crave, just like we all do. With God's blessing and colleagues at my side, my New Year's Resolution is simple: listen, notice, and remember.

SHARING THANKSGIVING

Holiday meals are upon us, and the pressure is mounting! Who to invite and what to serve? Add the commercial expectations of the perfectly laid table, and it's no wonder that most of us want to climb back in bed and hide under a blanket until the season is over.

Undaunted, I decided that Thanksgiving would be different this year. My in-town family was going out of town, so it was the perfect opportunity to shake things up a bit. In the past, I have taken turkey sandwiches to the streets and then returned home to eat. Why the arm's length relationship, I wondered? Why was I hesitant to ask homeless friends to come to my home and sit at my table? Did I worry that Harry would urinate on my velvet dining chairs or that

Thomas with his palsy hands would drop a crystal goblet? These excuses clouded the real reason I never invited them to sit at my table. I was embarrassed. In my former home, I had four bedrooms and five bathrooms for one person, me, while homeless "friends" slept outside and searched for restrooms.

I have downsized. It is humbling and humanizing all tangled together. Bless my homeless friends; they never judged, never remarked about the disparity between their home on the streets and mine, but I was bothered.

So this year I welcomed special guests and planned a menu. There was no brined turkey, just a good old Butterball bird with traditional sides of sweet potatoes with mini marshmallows, classic green bean casserole and homemade mashed potatoes with plenty of butter. My table was carefully laid with china, silver, and candles. Sounds of Vivaldi and the Mamas & the Papas filled my shotgun house.

I had to remember to consider the dental health of my guests (I have changed their names to protect their privacy). Harry has no teeth at all, Ben has a few, and Donna has jagged stumps with painful cavities. I served cider and lemonade, not alcohol. All of my guests battle personal demons, some have addiction problems, and several served jail time.

My protective older sister asked, "Are you afraid?" "Absolutely not," I replied, but then realized that despite hearing about these friends, her question highlighted the distance between homeless people and the general population.

On Thanksgiving, I rounded up my guests from various parts of the city. Robert, who spent most of his adult life in prison, resides in a trailer park. Donna and Harry, homeless for years, have small units in a housing project. Ben hunkers down between two stuffed shopping carts in an alley, and Michael's home is a rooftop. When we sat at the table, I asked if anyone wanted to offer a blessing.

Immediately everyone gripped hands tightly, and we formed a lopsided prayer circle amid the dinner plates and glasses. My guests offered words of gratitude followed by petitions: "Thank you God for getting me this far; I didn't believe it was possible." "Please God, do not abandon me as I still struggle." "Be with me always although I don't deserve a thing." My opening blessing seemed merely rote after listening to them, and I discovered that those who suffer the most offer the purest prayers from the heart.

Present-day Thanksgiving and Christmas celebrations rarely reflect the original events. Although the details of these historic happenings remain sketchy, we know that at the harvest festival of 1621, the Wampanoags and English colonists could not have been more different in their dress, food, and customs. The first Christmas was similarly diverse, the infant Son of God and his human family mingled with ignorant field workers who minded sheep and later with wealthy wise men who followed a star.

As a principal for many years who saw kindergartners make paper headdresses and Pilgrim hats for Thanksgiving feasts, and smiled as little boys in bathrobes became shepherds in nativity scenes, I should have grasped the message, but I got bogged down with specifics and swept up into the razzle-dazzle of the season.

Now I think I get it. It isn't about history, theology, or setting the perfect table. It's about family and friends, surely, but also about embracing the diversity of the original celebrants. It's about who I welcome into my home and into my heart.

NEEDING ONE ANOTHER

We couldn't be more different. He is Mexican-American, slight, handsome, and middle age. I am of Irish and Dutch descent, tall for a woman, and elderly. He has two years of formal schooling; I have twenty-two. He's lived in the woods, a bunk house, a shelter, a trailer, and a house. I have only lived in houses. He's been on his own since age seven, finding places to sleep, clothes to wear, and food to eat. At seven, I was driven to Brownie meetings, bribed to eat something green at family dinners, and tucked into bed each night. He's spent seventeen years in solitary confinement for committing a double homicide, has a record of seven aggravated assaults, and one charge of carrying a weapon. I have gotten two tickets for speeding, and one for making an illegal left turn.

So how did Diego (name changed to protect his privacy) and I, from two totally different worlds, become friends? We met at a small house-warming party in a trailer park, eyed each other awkwardly at first, and then struck up a conversation. It seemed almost at once that we needed each other. He needed work, and I needed someone to work... to trim bushes.

Thus, our relationship began. It was solidified early on when we spent hours sitting side-by-side on the unforgiving concrete of my driveway, trying to assemble a new electrical trimmer purchased for the job, with the deceptive words on the box, "easy assembly." We had to be a team because Diego could not read the directions well enough and I could not turn a screw tight enough.

That was years ago. Since then our relationship has evolved from friendship to fondness to love. Not the love between a man and a woman, but the love for another person on the planet who is placed in our path despite differences. Surely, there is a reason for this that we mortals cannot grasp.

Our friendship has been tested and transformed. Early on in our relationship Diego had to learn how to function outside prison walls and I had to grasp the enormity of the challenge. Health issues, a hip replacement coupled with periodic depression and anxiety attacks plague Diego. Ill prepared to offer any real help, I most often listen, encourage, and when really pressed suggest we pray together as we did on the phone once in the middle of the night while the police scoured the trailer park searching for him after a violent fight.

Diego is there for me as well, as true friends are. He's moved me from house to house to house, cleaned garages, planted flowers, and put together furniture (we both have gotten better at this)! He's decorated my Christmas tree, reminded me to buy gas when the gage gets low, and tried to warn me to stay out of what he considered dangerous neighborhoods when we delivered water, sandwiches, or day-old Starbuck's pastries to folks on the street.

One of our times together in Walmart, sort of says it all. Wandering through the home-decorating aisle, we discovered the display of essential oils, those tiny vials of scents, and debated... spring rain or sandalwood? And we agreed—never buy the overpowering midnight rose. This gift of enjoying each other simply and purely took my breath away as I thought about it much later—an ex-con and an old lady, a self-admitted addict and a school principal happily sharing a Martha Stewart moment. Only God could dream this up!

Diego didn't fear much, but he feared death. Not for any suffering involved, but because he believed he could not be forgiven for killing two men, one his brother. No God he thought could look the other way and say, "You are forgiven son." I tried to explain that he only had to be **truly sorry** and ask forgiveness. Diego wasn't ready to absorb this incredible idea. The timing of repentance is truly beyond our reach, which is why the death penalty is so wrong.

Our many faiths and laws say, thou shall not kill. And then we do—extinguishing any possible plea for mercy and a path to heaven.

How can this be?

FAITH

Person-to-person encounters are often the
turning points in a faith journey, and they
pop up where we least expect them.

FORTITUDE

Spring in Texas—torrential rains and flooding! Now summer's following suit, more rain, hurricane and tornado warnings, and possible flooding. I watch the weather channel and wonder if I have a working flashlight? Living alone, I try to be one step ahead of potential emergencies.

Today when the tornado watch is announced I text Emily, a friend who lives in a tiny, tinny trailer in an RV park and tell her it is one elderly woman checking up on another. I am older, but she is frailer and I worry about her. She has Chronic Obstructive Pulmonary Disease, COPD, and relies on oxygen for each breath. Her home is fragile also. Unlike my little shotgun house that has a foundation, hers is merely placed on a pad, not tethered down. A good gust of wind could carry it and her off easily. I know from news reports that mobile homes and their occupants are at serious risk in bad weather.

As good friends do, we comfort each other and realize in our back and forth text messages that we are both in our pajamas at noon, reading books while watching the pouring rain, guilty pleasures. We're two old tough birds making the most of a situation. Being alone and elderly requires a steady hand in life. Emily has had to dig deep to soldier on and she has. I am often in awe of her strength.

During long conversations we discover things in common: a love of Sky King in our childhood, memories of eating a standing rib roast dinner with our families, and Central Market, which Emily calls "another world of love." She also recalls an elegant evening with her mother and sister when they celebrated Christmas at the Four Seasons Hotel and enjoyed looking over the city lights of Houston.

How does one go from this fairy tale Christmas to being homeless and living in a tent on Riverside for 10 years? I have no answers, but know that Emily went from being a very competent corporate secretary to worrying about her safety and where her next meal would come from. She did plummet but she survived!

When I first knew Emily she was living in her trailer, and getting by quite well despite declining health. I was amazed at her tended garden and her trips to HEB on a red motorized scooter, a dangerous traffic-ladened journey of several miles. She never complained, relishing her little home and independence.

Emily had a New England style reflecting her roots. She wore flowered dresses and her hair in a long thick braid. A woman's hair is said to be her crowning glory, and I have witnessed a crushing change in my friend. She first cut off her braid. "Too difficult to maintain," she said, and recently had her head shaved to eliminate even the demands of caring for short hair. With dignity and a remarkable lack of self-pity, she presses on. I am the one depressed by this radical step of some femininity lost.

With each breath a struggle, Emily is now house-bound. A home health-care aide comes several days a week to help with the basics of daily living. A cat and her books keep her company and, at night, although she doesn't comment, her fears must be magnified. The dark makes being old, alone, and ill a formidable challenge.

Emily shared some of her secrets for coping. She reads a card given to her at St. David's Hospital which has prayers for every faith. The words comfort her. She realizes we all praise God and ask for help in similar ways. She also says the rosary. Although Emily is not a Catholic, several months ago she asked me to teach her how to pray the rosary. I was delighted. We began to pray together. On the first bead of the first decade of beads, she said, "Slow down, I need to think about what I am saying." Being a life-long Catholic, I was used to rushing from bead to bead, barely comprehending what I was saying or doing. Slow down, show reverence, relish the moment— more lessons learned from this woman of faith and fortitude.

WE ARE CALLED

Sometimes simple pleasures are the best—like introducing two of my friends to each other, believing that they would delight in each other and discovering they did! Bishop Emeritus John McCarthy sat in a shelter one evening visiting with the guests. A spirit-filled man with a soft spot for those who are down and out, I knew my friend David would enjoy meeting the Bishop. I located David in the crowd and said, "Come, there is someone I want you to meet." Once the perfunctory introductions were made, I left them alone knowing I was not needed to cement this relationship.

Later, Bishop John told me that David said, "Bishop, I feel called by God." Bishop John in his wisdom said, "Son, we are all called by God." I surmise that what David was saying was that perhaps he was being called to the religious life. Bishop reminded David and all of us really, that we are called to be the best we can be, to model Christ in whatever vocation we choose.

David lives in a tent in the woods. He works several days a week doing manual labor: cutting grass, painting, cleaning up stadium seating, and hauling trash. His days are measured not by these tasks, but by time spent in adoration before the Blessed Sacrament. A distinctive and essential doctrine of the Catholic Church is that the bread and wine consecrated at Mass truly become the "real presence" of the body of Christ. Believers hold this transubstantiation sacred. In Catholic churches at certain times, the consecrated hosts are taken from the locked tabernacle and placed in a monstrance (a designated vessel) for adoration. This is where David wants to be each day. He is mindful of which church has exposition and adoration and at what time so he does not miss being present.

On and off since 2000, I have been head of a Catholic School so I have had the opportunity to attend Mass frequently, participate in liturgies, and be surrounded by holy men and women. In this rich spiritual milieu, my faith has grown far beyond anything I ever imagined. When I am around David, however, I am a neophyte, a catechumen who despite plowing through St. Thomas Aquinas' *Summa Theologica* in college, with thousands of paper-thin pages filled with dense theology, I feel I know nothing. Any faith I have pales in comparison to David's. He is on fire with love for the Lord and has said "Prayer saved me." When we are together, we say the rosary. He always has one, I rarely do, so I just hold his hand that holds the beads and we pray the decades reverently in one voice.

I know nothing of David's past life, and it really doesn't matter, but he assures me it was a mess. In his words, "He misused God's gifts." When we reconnected recently he reminded me that I fed him on the streets. I don't remember as there are many homeless men and women needing food and so much more. We were brought together this time for a purpose, I believe. He to inspire me, to strengthen my faith, a pastoral purpose of enormous proportions and my task, to tutor him in English so he can pass the high school equivalency exam. Next to his daily adoration, getting his GED is paramount to him.

Back to the conversation with my wise friend Bishop John. Isn't this what we are all trying to figure out? Is God calling us? Surely He must be. He loves us so much he speaks to each one of us, sometimes with a whisper and sometime with a shout. I was never sure how this miracle happened and then discovered that God talks to us in many ways, through prayer, reading, adoration, and through people, His special messengers.

Our job is to listen with an open heart, ready with humility and gratitude for what comes our way, acknowledging that we are perpetual pilgrims who rarely know the route of our journey even if we think we do. There is no GPS to heaven, well maybe there is—"Love one another as I have loved you."

THE GOOD THIEF

He mentioned in passing that he had stolen more than 100 guns. This was a sub plot in the midst of a discussion about Bible verses. Then Tomas asked me to read a piece he had written, which I did. What amazed me at first was his incredible handwriting. It was actually stylized printing similar to what a trained architect would use to solidify ideas and intrigue others. It was a full page of sentences artfully arranged on unlined paper. There was flow, originality, and passion in the writing.

I sensed that this man needed to be heard, so I listened. His work was basically commentary on certain Bible verses. Maybe this was my path into the sub plot—stolen guns. So I asked him, "How did you get so familiar with the Bible?" And he said, "I spent four years in a maximum security prison cell where I ate, slept, showered, and relieved myself. While I was there, I read the Bible six times front to back, Genesis through Revelation."

When Tomas asked me, "What is your favorite chapter in the Bible?" I stumbled, not used to this probing question and mumbled, "I'm not sure." Clearly I was out of my realm with him biblically and had not even thought of a favorite chapter. In truth, I had never read the entire book. He kindly glossed over my sketchy response and told me his favorite was Ecclesiastes.

Saying this, he went to his backpack and dug out his, carefully protected in a plastic bag to keep it dry and pointed out favorite verses. His Bible was not leather bound or gold embossed, nor did it have any artist's renderings, but he had found it, it was now his and precious to him. Reading through the good book six times in prison changed this man it seems.

Tomas must have battled discrimination in the past and even now, for he is not one who radiates a presence. He has missing teeth, a mild stutter and his appearance is a mite seedy. Although hesitant in manner, Tomas is determined in spirit and presses on. His past both weighs him down and lifts him up.

Persistent criminal behavior and repeated robberies of firearms were products of who knows what, but Tomas admits to drug and alcohol abuse. When we talked he had gone 22 days without using drugs and 17 days without smoking cigarettes. He knows that he can get drugs, alcohol, and cigarettes if he weakens, but he ignores what is around him and focuses on the Bible and his writing.

We read in the gospels of Matthew, Mark, Luke, and John that two criminals were crucified alongside Christ. According to biblical scholars these two thieves must have done something beyond petty stealing, which usually resulted in being stoned to death. Being crucified was reserved for the most heinous of crimes. Along with those present at the crucifixion of Christ, these two robbers hurled insults at Jesus as they hung on either side of him.

Then we read a startling account in Luke. "One of the criminals who was hanged railed at him, saying, 'Are you not the Christ? Save yourself and us!' But the other rebuked him saying, 'Do you not fear God, since you are under the same sentence of condemnation? And we indeed justly; for we are receiving the due reward of our deeds; but this man has done nothing wrong.' And he said, 'Jesus remember me when you come into your kingdom.' And he said to him, 'Truly, I say to you, today you will be with me in Paradise." Luke 23 39:43

I wonder, is Tomas today's good thief? He and the good thief in the Bible, who was nameless, but traditionally is referred to as Dismas by some Christians, both had a change of heart. They repented and the mercy of God prevailed.

Our choices then and now are simple: can we admit our guilt, can we accept punishment, and can we ask for forgiveness. If we can, love might save us.

Two thieves, outcasts and outlaws—Dismas saved by Christ himself. Tomas saved by a holy book. How strangely wonderful.

SURFACE IMPRESSIONS

David called to say that he had hauled gravel the day before, found a place to pitch his tent in the woods, and had just gone to Mass. He relocated to another state in search of something new and a full week's work. In his prior job, with the health insurance requirements, his employer cut David's minimum wage position to three days a week and did so to others so he would not have to pay insurance. What should have helped these folks backfired!

For the past year, David has lived on a church campus between buildings where there is an overhang to shelter him from the rain. He is a squatter and arrives late when the service and activities are over, and leaves in the dark before being noticed. This system worked pretty well until recently. Like many other homeless people, he uses a friend's place for the occasional shower and sometimes between these clean-ups looks a little scruffy with a black beard trying to take hold. Under his shirt is always a cross.

Andy lives on the streets and carries his belongings in bulging shopping bags wherever he goes, including daily Mass. He is an Anglo fluent in Spanish, learned while serving a prison term by reading two editions of the Bible, set side-by-side, one in English and one in Spanish. He has no ID, job, or place to live, nevertheless he reads books on faith and recommends St. Francis' story of perfect joy, from *The Little Flower of St. Francis* to a recent convert to Catholicism. The message somehow gives meaning to Andy's life—that true joy comes not from success or earthly happiness, but rather from focusing on Christ even while enduring defeat, suffering, and rejection.

Boston Chris survives by dumpster-diving. He has found some amazing toss-a-ways, including a gold medal, which he took to a place that buys gold. Delighted with its worth, he pocketed some of the cash and gave the rest to a friend. But his specialty is academic books. After each college semester, he knows the best places to sort through dumpsters in search of text books that have been tossed. He knows the value of most and appreciates the heavy medical or legal volumes. He too is a church-goer and usually arrives early to grab his favorite seat in the corner of the last row.

What do we see when we look at these men—perhaps an uncomfortableness in their alien lifestyle. They have no resumes or recommendations from prior work. They have no degrees. They have no long-term goals. They function in the here and now. The daily or maybe weekly agenda is as far as they venture. They trust in the generosity of friends, the majority being just like them, and the eternal goodness of God. Clothing, food, shelter, and hygiene fluctuate depending upon small sums earned, the kindness of strangers, the availability of community and faith-based programs for the poor, and their own ingenuity.

Beneath the surface, which may be difficult to ignore, these men, and so many others like them are faith-filled worshippers. Why? I believe it is because they have no one else to turn to when they are lonely, hungry, or sick, but to a God who says He loves them. And they believe it.

We can get smug—when we have the mortgage payments planned out, a nearly full refrigerator, credit cards, a wallet with some cash, a button to press for warm or cool air, a comfy bed, and a family. We think we are squared away and not in any desperate need of a supernatural force—a God who loves us no matter what.

Jesus, the son of God as Christians believe, traveled by foot, slept outside or in a room that was offered, accepted the hospitality of strangers for food, and endured heat, cold, loneliness at times, and rejection by many. No wonder, David, Andy, Boston Chris and so many other homeless people identify with Jesus. He is one of them.

We who are smug, sometimes need an unexpected incident in our lives—illness, suffering, or loss—to inch closer to Christ like these holy men.

SLEEPING WITH JESUS

At age 70 it's been more than a decade since I slept next to a man, close enough to feel our breath fan each other's face. Thus, the intimacy seemed staggering. My first instinct was to turn over to protect this intrusion of personal space and cherished memory of sharing long ago. Fortunately, some childhood ingrained politeness took over and cautioned, don't be rude, stay put, welcome this. And so I did for one long cold night lying mere inches away from a homeless man.

Earlier, I had selected my sleeping spot for the night on a sidewalk next to a church wall that I thought might protect me from the cold currents swirling through the parking lot. JD who knew me from the streets asked if he could sleep next to me, "to block the wind" he said.

Truthfully, I outweighed him by 40 pounds and should have been sleeping on the outside, but he was the grace-filled one.

It was in the high thirties this Austin night. Somewhat experienced in sleeping on the streets, I thought I was prepared. Wearing two shirts, a wind-blocking vest and fleece jacket, a hat and mittens, I was almost ready to fight the chill. A last-minute addition to my backpack and wardrobe, fuzzy pajama bottoms, basic black with frolicsome pink and blue bunnies, were pulled on over my pants before bedding down and got nary a snicker from the homeless folks. They knew warmth was in, fashion was out.

Sadly, the newly purchased less-than-ten-dollars sleeping bag I brought was no steal. Its glossy red surface smacking of star performance unfortunately had hit-and-miss stuffing and the zipper put up a fight as soon as my mittened hands tried to engage it. With me inside, two homeless friends had to push and pull vigorously to get the zipper to cooperate ever so slightly. Contemplating this I thought, if I have to escape in a hurry, I will have to hop; there is no alternative in this modern day mummy-wrap.

Once inside the bag, I folded a scarf and fashioned a sort of pillow. My sleep partner said, "Is that all you have for your head?" I replied, "Yes" whereupon he dug into his backpack and pulled out several items of clothing that he assured me were clean, these he carefully folded and placed under my scarf for a newly cushioned head rest.

As the noises of the city abated a bit and the night wore on, we snuggled as best we could in our separate, but coupled sleeping bags. For the final night-time preparation, JD wrapped a well-used blanket around both of the bags creating a sort of womb for just us two. Throughout the night whenever I moved even a smidgen, I felt a big hand reach out and tenderly re-tuck me inside the blanket. The continuum of care was astounding as I floated between muted states of slumber and wakefulness.

A wise and holy man once said when I went out on the streets—I should look for the face of Jesus Christ in those I met. That cold and windy night, it registered. JC, a homeless, probably hungry at times, and undoubtedly often weary God-Man chose JD, another homeless, hungry, weary man, to embody his love. Seeing beyond what was, I somehow sensed I was sleeping with Jesus. He was the Good Shepherd looking for me in this city jungle and upon finding me, sheltered me with gentleness. It was his thin body that blocked the wind; it was his hands that lovingly touched mine. And, when I woke during the night, it was his face I saw illuminated by the street lights, a face lined with worry, making my heart ache. Ultimately, it was his sweet smile radiating forgiveness even in sleep that gave me hope. The night wore on, the cold wind howled, it suddenly didn't matter. In the everyday world of miracles, when we least expect it, Christ comes to us, not on billowing clouds with trumpets blaring, but oh so simply and quietly through each other. A reassuring revelation of His humanity, Jesus snores.

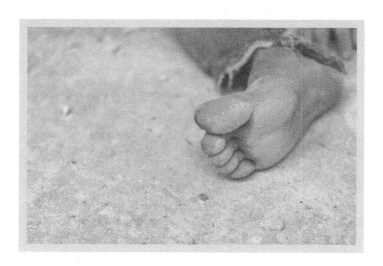

THE BOTTOM OF THE BARREL

This was dropped in my lap as I cruised along in my newly leased upscale, all powerful, shiny vehicle that knows more than I do. The radio was doing its thing in the background. It was just white noise until these words leaped out at me—"You will find God in the bottom of the barrel."

Barrel? What barrel—yesterday's barrel, today's barrel? Whose barrel?

The bottom of my barrel? As I battle bronchitis for four weeks? As I grieve for my younger brother by five years who died last month? As I realize that my son is more fragile than I am as a senior citizen. Will I find God here?

The bottom of your barrel? As I hear about a house that has not sold and the family is frantic. As I witness friends dueling with political swords and wounding each other gravely. As I talk to a woman in public housing who juggles bills like a Las Vegas dealer trying to decide what gets attention—the phone company, the utility company, the empty dog dish? Will I find God here?

The bottom of our barrel? As I realize that there is a man without legs who lives under the overpass, alone with his cardboard bed and Bible. As I watch once joyful relationships fade and die. As I try to navigate our new world with a divided nation, violence erupting in cities, and foreign countries fighting over land, religious dominance, and economic control. Will I find God here?

I am a master of out of sight out of mind. Denial and escape are secret coping mechanisms for me and many of us, I suspect. In an imagined rain barrel full of water, the things that rise to the top grab my attention. These are the buoyant beautiful things that make me smile. So, I buy Christmas presents—toys for my young grandchildren and the new Glimmer Strings LED lights for the rest of the family. I relish Christmas carols and sing along. I bask in the banks of poinsettias and sparkling trees in church surrounding the manger scene. These are the easy things to grab and hold on to from my barrel.

For me, for you, for us, the buoyant beautiful things that float to the top of a rain barrel are much the same—new gadgets, sports, pets, parties, friends and family, entertainment, laughter, home, vehicles, food, celebrations, and the internet.

Am I messing around with these lovelies floating to the top, because I am reluctant to dig deeper to the bottom of the barrel where the force of gravity drags down things with weight? Here debris settles, the muck is thick, and everything is not so lovely. If I am brave enough to dig with bare hands, will I see the ugliness, the pain, the anger, the loneliness of the people unlike me and like me at the bottom? Will I see God as promised on the radio?

I know I avoid peering into the darkness at the bottom of the barrel because it is just too much to bear. It demands excruciating focus on things I'd rather dismiss as not mine. Still I hear the man on the radio saying: "You will find God in the bottom of the barrel" so I push myself and wonder ...

Why did I walk past the person sleeping on the sidewalk with a bare foot sticking out of a dirty blanket while I hurried past to a fancy restaurant doing nothing, not even covering the foot in the freezing air?

Why did I hunker down at home and fret about my own minor illness, forgetting about those in hospitals, nursing homes, and hospice facilities?

Why did I paper over my personal failings while noticing and criticizing the arrogance and errors of others?

Why did I let impermanent things, the gifts, the lights, and the music woo me into mere amusement?

Still I'm trying. So I dig down almost to the bottom of the barrels—yours, mine, ours—finding rubble, wreckage, agony, despair, sickness, injury, brokenness, filth, lies, selfishness, abandonment, and trash.

Now I'm digging deeper where there is guilt, forgiveness, and hope.

And I'm finding God.

PRAYER

Prayer is not an add-on in our lives;
it is the essential conversation.

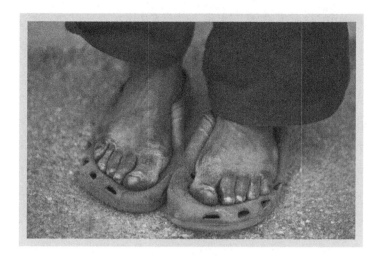

ON MY KNEES

Kneeling was not my thing. Although I was a regular churchgoer, I had perfected the art of pseudo-kneeling. By putting my knees on the edge of the kneeler while the bulk of my body weight rested on the pew, I pretended. Thank God I was given another chance to know what it really means to be on my knees in prayer.

In 2000 I moved to Austin to become head of St. Gabriel's Catholic School. The Director of Religious Education asked if during Holy Week, I would be willing to wash the feet of twelve people chosen from the school community to represent the apostles. I felt honored, then humbled, and ultimately panicked. I didn't know how to do this, and worried not just about the practical "how to's," but about the meaning of being a servant, a foot washer in public.

This foot washing ritual initially made me wonder, "Is this too personal?" "Who washes feet and whose feet get washed?" and "What is the meaning of all this?" History helped here.

Going barefoot, or wearing sandals, was common in ancient times. Foot washing was a sign of hospitality, a practical gesture assigned to the lowliest servant who washed away dirt from a visitor's feet. Jesus had his feet washed by others upon entering their homes as was the custom, but more amazing to His apostles—He got down on His knees and washed their feet at the last supper, saying, "As I have done to you, so you do also." I focused on this literally at first, forgetting it is the symbolism that speaks so eloquently.

For eight years in a row, I celebrated Holy Thursday at St. Gabriel's on my knees slowly moving on a carpeted stage from person to person. Assisted by altar servers holding pressed towels and warm water in earthenware pitchers, I washed feet. Each foot I held and poured water over was treasured. Every face I looked into inspired me to tell them they were loved by God. These middle-class feet whether young or old were un-scarred, almost perfect.

Several years later, I found myself on my knees in a far different setting, this time at Mission Possible, on the East Side. After a fellowship dinner, several of us who had been on a street retreat offered to wash the feet of homeless guests. We knelt on the crumbling linoleum floor in front of each person on a folding chair. There was no system; we just moved about the crowd gently asking, "May I wash your feet?" Whispers of "Yes" were sometimes mingled with tears. An unmistakable reverence surfaced. Runners filled plastic pitchers again and again and our kitchen towels grew damp from use. It took courage for these men to show their street-worn, sometimes washed feet to a woman. It took equal courage for me to look at those abused feet with blistered skin and blackened nails. Some feet were so swollen I had to peel socks off and brace myself for what was beneath, but our shared vulnerability let love surface.

Just a year ago during Holy Week, I washed feet in a downtown alley. Homeless folks getting ready to bed down on concrete were cautious when I said, "May I wash your feet?" They had never been invited to share in this way, some agreed. Recycled dumpster cardboard placed over the rough blacktop defined our prayer space. Restaurant supply pitchers filled with water and rag tag towels were at the ready. Sirens and other street sounds became our sacred night music. Being in an alley made this foot washing unique almost freeform, yet most people knew something special was happening.

The beauty of this ritual, I eventually realized, is its simplicity. When I knelt down before another, in submission, I was imitating Christ. The people allowing me to wash their feet surrendered Christ-like as well, for feet, the work-horse team of the body show wear. In this profoundly moving exchange, I was shown that real prayer is all about a willingness to serve and be served, to love and be loved.

Where will I kneel this year to receive the grace of the season, I wonder?

PRAY FOR ME

Lenny sat on the stoop of an abandoned building slowly munching a bologna and cheese sandwich I had just given him. It was a Friday night in the bustling club section of the city filled with street sounds and laughter. The people all around us were gearing up for the weekend, happy to put the work-week behind them. Singles on the lookout, couples hand-in-hand, and boisterous small groups hurried in and out of bars hoping to get a good seat or hear some rocking music. These "suits" (people with jobs) smacked of pride and promise. Lenny, on the other hand, was not part of this world, nor were the other homeless folks wandering downtown. He watched the "suits" as I did and then it seemed we were both struck by the incongruity of it all—the haves and the have-nots, the hopefuls and the hopeless, living on different planets almost, yet all within an arm's reach. Lenny turned to me not with malice or envy, but with desperation and said quietly, "Pray for me, please"—a plea impossible to ignore.

There have always been people who have done this kind of holy work, praying for others. Various contemplative orders of the Catholic Church such as the Carmelites and the Trappists believe that this is what they are called to do—dedicate their lives to praying for the world while living simple lives, often in cloistered communities. For some people, this may seem irrelevant useless work; to contemplatives, it is holy work that they feel privileged to do.

Norman R. Davies, a religious Jew living a contemplative lifestyle in Spain blogs, "As Jews, we accept that our petitionary prayer is always conditional upon the will of God. We are not spiritual wizards or cosmic manipulators." Deceased Catholic theologian, former contemplative, and prolific writer Henri J.M. Nouwen states in *With Open Hands* that prayer, if it is real, is suffused with hope, "it is not a question of having a wish come true but of expressing an unlimited faith in the giver of all good things." He adds, "Whenever we pray and leave out our neighbors, our prayer is not real prayer."

I am a lay practitioner in this prayer business, yet many of us who are parents or grandparents discover prayer naturally when children enter our lives. By some miraculous process, when we have a child, our ego takes a back seat, which must be the essence of parenting. It is not even an act of will, it just happens to most of us, the child comes first in all things including our prayers and we find ourselves saying simple prayers out of gratitude or desperation. "Thank you God for this beautiful baby." "Please God, keep Charlie safe as he drives alone for the first time." If we are truly honest and humble, the overwhelming responsibility of raising a child whom we love without measure, makes prayer an inescapable pathway in parenting.

So, although a novice, I press on. When I go about my day and really notice people in my world—the dad carrying his handicapped child into the coffee shop, the woman crossing the busy intersection using her breath to control the wheelchair—spontaneous prayer for them is on my lips. When I go to bed at night, I try to remember those in most need of prayer and by name, ask God to bless them and strengthen them in their struggles. The list contains a few standards, family and friends, but changes constantly as people like Lenny briefly become part of my life.

God being all knowing and all loving understands what's in our hearts, so what does this praying really mean? I think it means that we become changed by thinking of others in this very intimate manner. When we get out of our own stumbling, bumbling, ego-centric way and think of others first, our prayers go from "Help me" to "Help them," a big step in becoming more human, more holy. Each little prayer is a gracious, selfless moment, bringing us closer to the kind of person we are called to be. Bless you Lenny for inviting me to pray. You will not be forgotten.

RAMADAN

He stood off to the side, holding his plastic bag of food, watching other men from the half-way house waiting in line. Long and lean and looking different from the rest in a freshly pressed tan shirt buttoned from top collar to hem, pink polaroid sunglasses, and a grey well-tended pony tail, he caught my eye.

I walked over to him and said, "You look very handsome." He smiled and said, "Will you marry me?" "I need to know your name first," I replied. He said, "William is my first name." "Fine name" I said and added, "Let me think about the proposal okay?" William smiled another sweet smile. There we were on a hot June evening, two senior citizens gently reaching out to each other, exchanging pleasantries, and flirting in the most innocent way.

We both really understood the situation. He was an ex-convict, recently released from prison and I was handing out free food to men in the parking lot of a half-way house. When I mentioned his stylish shades, he mumbled something about needing them, so I never saw his eyes, the doorway to the soul, but the casual comment about needing the sunglasses and seeing his shirt buttoned tightly despite the heat made me wonder if he had some prison abuse or tat to hide.

William was looking for a job in a fast food restaurant and had been to Goodwill Industries to see if there were any openings. Driving a forklift was his goal—there were no positions. Together we discussed how important it was to be willing to start at the bottom in a job search. William was not proud and said he would do most anything for a real job. I agreed with his thinking, yet anyone eavesdropping would be suspect just looking at us and hearing our conversation, for to the outside world, we were two elderly and somewhat frail folks who probably could not haul trays of food all day or work a forklift endlessly.

William wanted to move out of the half-way house with its bed bugs and series of men coming and going, so he needed work to be able to get a place of his own. And he declared, "I'm not going back to prison. I did a dumb thing once and learned my lesson."

After these initial exchanges, things got serious. William asked if I had a faith? He could not tell as I wear no cross, it rests hidden in my heart. I responded, "Yes Christian—Catholic." He said, "I am a Muslim, and as people of faith, we are required to respect each other." I asked if he prayed five times a day, and he said, "Yes."

Because I still use a paper calendar, I knew that Ramadan was beginning that next Monday, June 6th, and ending July 5th. We discussed the feast, the most holy month for Muslims where they fast—no eating, drinking, or smoking during daylight—as prayer and sacrifice. According to Robin Scher, a freelance writer from South Africa, during Ramadan in 2016, an estimated 1.6 billion Muslims around the world will be celebrating their religion's most sacred month. "Fasting," he adds, "helps to build compassion and empathy for the less fortunate, who may not always have the freedom to choose not to eat. By fasting, Muslims remind themselves what it means to experience hunger and thirst." Something William probably understands firsthand without fasting, yet he will fast.

From a food truck run to a half-way house, an ex-convict recently released from prison and a former school principal connect. Beginning with compliments on attire and talks of marriage—harmless bantering—comes more powerful dialogue and meaning. We discuss that if we are people of faith, any faith, we are beholden to honor each other. Lent for Christians, Ramadan for Muslims, consist of deep beliefs, sacrifice, prayer, and fasting.

Tragically, in the past, and certainly today extremists can be found in any faith. These are those who have lost their way and believe they are little gods—belittling, exploiting, and harming others. For William and me, the essence of our faith is worshiping the one true God wholeheartedly and loving our neighbor.

MY TWO JOHNS

I met "My Two Johns" when they were in bed. John #1 was in a hospital at the tail end of a July 4th weekend. In pain, he feared appendicitis. Within a short time it was determined that this was more serious. He had a mass in his colon and was facing surgery in the morning. Fearing the worst, he wanted a priest to give him Holy Communion. Given the holiday, a priest was not to be found in the hospital or for a time anywhere else. A friend who knew of the situation called me and asked if I could bring the Eucharist to this young man. When I determined that it was his request and not that of his parents, I said, "Yes, give me a few minutes."

With a quick change from casual clothes and a gas tank fill-up, I arrived at the hospital and ran into Father Bud Roland, pastor of St. John Neumann Catholic Church. He too was summoned and we both discovered that neither one of us knew the patient. Together we hurried through the hospital labyrinth to his room. There he was in bed surrounded by his young wife, his siblings and their significant others, his parents, and old family friends. Immediately, I went to John and said, "I am here for you." Father Bud assumed pastoral leadership and we circled John's bed in prayer. Honest emotions, heart-felt pleas combined with hopeful outcomes for John's health charged the air of the small space we occupied. It was surreal. When it ended, I felt privileged to be part of this intimate prayerful family gathering. Sometime later I was informed that John survived the surgery, had colon cancer, and was to undergo chemotherapy.

John #2 was flat on his back as well when I first saw him. His bed was a city bench. Wrapped in blankets head to toe and covered in newspapers, I was not even sure that under that sizeable lump was a person. I pulled my car into a parking lot, walked up to the bench and said, "Hello." There was no reply. So I left a large chocolate chip cookie on a party napkin by his bed and wondered who this sleeping giant was. I returned again and again, hoping to meet him. Finally one day, he opened one eye and said, "Hi." Then he asked, "Are you the one who leaves the treats?" I admitted I was. Our relationship was very formal at this point. He slept on the bench covered in layers with only his mouth visible and I kept visiting, not waking him, but leaving a donut or a muffin or a cookie on a party napkin.

Eventually John moved from bench to alley. Still bundled in layers, he slept inside a cardboard box and kept his valuables in an overflowing shopping cart. With time we began to talk, mostly centered on general topics, the weather and how we both were. He had serious skin problems and rarely wore shoes; I had a critically ill son. Perhaps our pain bonded us, talking led to hugging and seeing each other brought joy. John began each conversation selflessly asking, "How is your son?" Although strangers for some time, we gradually began to care deeply for each other.

Today, "My Two Johns" are doing well. John #1 is finished with chemotherapy, cancer free, and back at work. John #2 has gotten an apartment in a city home. Both men feared death for different reasons, one from cancer and the other from a ravaged life on the streets. Instead, they found God's tender loving mercy waiting for them in the wings. There are so many ways to love and be loved. Each instance, each relationship is an invitation to live more fully and welcome grace as it comes our way.

This all began with John #1 wanting to receive the Eucharist and I remember discovering that Eucharist means thanksgiving. Recently I've been humming a favorite hymn, "Make us a Eucharistic people, in everything we are … ." Inspired by the lyrics and "My Two Johns," I'm now whispering again and again the purest prayer of all, "Thank you."

SAM DIED TODAY

Sam died today. I see this one-line memorial on the home page of my computer when I boot up and my breath catches. Nearly a year ago I placed this electronic headstone on my southwestern wallpaper scene. Sam's cyberspace cemetery, courtesy of Google's design, is a brightly colored stucco wall adorned with dried chilies hanging from a hand-crafted ladder. I think putting him here was my way of marking a life, so I wouldn't forget.

Sam died in an alley I was told. Feelings of unexplained loss merged with flashbacks of his life. His gap-toothed grin was magical. After 63 years on this earth fighting for dignity and for some small share of our bounty, he was ever hopeful. Occasional work in a garage made

Sam feel useful and helped fund his few valuables, such as the tiny TV he treasured.

Friends in the park gave him a much needed sense of community. Sam was charismatic, often the gracious one to help and delighted in doing so. The first day I met him, something clicked and we knew we would be friends forever. While I was offering sandwiches to hungry folks from the back of my truck, Sam sprang into action, picking up debris on the ground, shaking out crumbs from a plastic table cloth laid over the tail-gate, and restoring food bins to order. We were a seamless team from then on, waiter and bus person, happily serving our customers.

News traveled fast—"Sam died of a drug overdose." Distressed by this shocking turn of events, I had to see for myself and try to make sense of it. From bits and pieces of street gossip, all I knew was that Sam was found in an alley behind a yellow gas station on the East Side. Armed with this sketchy information, I set out to discover where he lived and where he died.

While cruising up and down Seventh Street and wandering along various side roads, I spotted a man sitting alone on a curb, his feet planted firmly in the gutter. After offering him water, I sat down to join him. He was gracious and spoke easily when I asked if he knew Sam. He did. Confirming the rumors, he said, "Yes, Sam died suddenly during the night behind a garage where he often worked. It's close by." Guided by this gentleman's directions, I found the alley where Sam lived and spent his last night. My friend's death suddenly became real.

A handful of us went to the King Tears funeral home to pay our respects. He looked magnificent laid out in a coffin, regal really in a dark pin-striped suit and red tie. Surprisingly, it cheered us to see Sam this way, looking better in death than in life.

We signed our names in the mortuary book, said a prayer together, and walked back to my car wiping away tears. Our visiting team was unusual, a homeless woman I didn't know well who dressed up for the occasion, a street friend who just this once left his overflowing shopping cart, and me, a woman with a home. Sam brought us together this day as we honored him and heard whispers of our own mortality; your time is coming also.

Maybe this is what real friends and families do, stick by each other in good times and bad, and when death comes, those who die first serve as the anointed messengers of our own forthcoming demise. Without these stark reminders, we skirt around the obvious—life ends in death.

Did Sam have a family? I've no idea. Where was he from? I don't know. Why was he part of my world? I'm not sure. Could it be that for a brief time, I would be swept into his spirit-filled life; which might have seemed empty to many, but to me seemed radiant and full of grace? Could it be that his death was more meaningful than his life, reminding us, his friends, that we too could die suddenly, and perhaps alone, in the dark? There are no answers. I only know that Sam's passing leaves a hole in my heart. Lord have mercy.

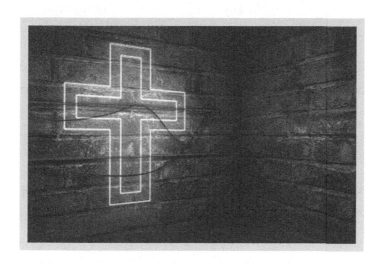

FORGIVENESS

I'm looking for a sign to hang in my house, "Forgive everyone everything," not because I'm advertizing sainthood, quite the contrary. My faults are ever-present and embarrassing. Needing constant reminders of what's important in life, I feel a sign might help me forgive and forget the petty annoyances that pepper my day-to-day life. Since I'm a closet Martha Stewart, the sign should be tasteful I think and complement my décor. Okay, on the other hand it should probably glow in the dark or have neon blinking lights to grab my attention.

My list of annoyances is long. Yesterday the man in front of me in the supermarket express line had a full cart, enough to feed a family of five. My pulse quickened; my blood pressure spiked. Looking at his overloaded cart and then at the sign, *Limit 10 Items*, my distain was noticeable. Later I wondered, why couldn't I just accept what was? He may have had a reason for ignoring the system or maybe he just wasn't a rule follower. At any rate I magnified the situation although no one else was even bothered.

Something else happened recently that irked me; on I-35 the driver behind me in the next lane wouldn't let me in when the lanes merged. He just gunned it and glared at me as if the diminishing lanes were my fault. Even though he couldn't hear me at that point, I shouted "Thanks a lot!"

And then, settling into my favorite neighborhood Starbucks after a long work day, the woman in the comfy leather chair across from me proceeded to read the newspaper out loud. I wanted to scream. Each word was slowly enunciated until she moved on to the next, meanwhile I was gradually going mad. Completely forgetting that this was a public place, my self-righteousness surged, meanwhile compassion took a back seat as I huffed and puffed over a beginning adult reader who had a right to read anyway she liked in public.

It has been said that confession is good for the soul, so here goes. I am impatient and judgmental. I want my world to function well and on my terms. This is how I get by. Looking back on these examples I realize that all of the annoyances in my life are really irrelevant, small inconveniences, but still I'm testy inside. Age has not produced the wisdom authors write about so eloquently in poems and stories.

My behavior is pretty scary because I realize that basically my life has been a series of blessings. No brutality has touched it nor have mistakes of my fellow man required a pardon on my part. In more contemplative moments, I wonder how I would react if this were not so? Would I retaliate against violence or would I, Gandhi-like, turn the other cheek? If my present posture is any indication, beware world!

When I moved to Austin, my first friend was Monsignor Richard McCabe, a feisty match to my fire if ever there was one, which is perhaps why we got along so well. He was a creative risk-taker who founded Caritas, as well as Lakeway Ecumenical Church and Emmaus Catholic Church. He believed "No" was a distasteful word and as a result ruffled a few feathers. One day after lunching together he said, "Come see what I am giving to _____" (a foe). A carefully wrapped family heirloom rested in the back seat of his car.

I was astonished and said, "Sport" (my nickname for him) "How can you give that treasure to someone who caused you so much grief?" Enlightenment can come with old age I then discovered because he turned to me and said, "Judy, forgiveness is all that matters." Monsignor's normally disguised saintliness startled me and changed me. Not wanting to waste this wisdom gift, I continued my search for the perfect sign.

Then kaboom, no more searching, I figured it out. The cross is the perfect sign for "Forgive everyone everything" and imagine Jesus adding, "I did, and still do, if only you ask."

Like city mission churches with crosses that flicker on and off all night beckoning lost souls, I probably need to go neon.

GRACE

Grace-filled moments don't come at our
bidding. They are gifts in the truest sense and
seem the surest proof of the existence of God.
While we don't summon these moments, we
have to be ready to host them.

IT WAS A BLUSTERY DAY

It was a blustery winter day. The wind whipped about spiraling dry leaves and paper scraps everywhere. As I searched for a close-in parking space in the enormous Walmart lot, I glanced at the temperature gage, 35 degrees. The near freezing conditions and dark clouds overhead made it feel like snow or mixed precipitation as the weather forecasters like to say. After hunting for my gloves, I wrapped my fleece jacket around me tightly, and hurried from my car to the entrance of the store.

Near the door, an old woman wrapped in a light shawl sat on a wooden bench waiting. Her dark eyes seemed to pierce right through me. Then she spoke, "Please Dearie, can you spare some change for a pair of britches? I have none." I was completely taken aback, embarrassed for her, embarrassed for me, and embarrassed for passersby who might have heard this uniquely intimate plea. My imagination went wild for a few moments. I tried to figure out how this could be! Was she raped? Were her underclothes so ripped that they were beyond repair? Were they soiled? After a few minutes of this free-range panicking, I realized it really didn't matter, the fact remained that under her skirt she was wearing nothing!

Over the years panhandlers have asked for money, a hamburger, dog food, or coffee, but no one has ever pleaded for this basic necessity—underwear. How desperate she must have been to beg, feeling exposed and totally stripped of human dignity.

Flustered, I handed her five dollars. She thanked me and went inside. Although I am usually comfortable being around poor and homeless people, this felt awkward and I didn't know how to react. My first thought after she went inside was purely practical and ridiculously focused on fashion. I worried that she would never find "britches" in there. The underwear aisles as I recalled had packages of lace thongs, neon bright bikinis, and rainbow-hued hipster panties designed for the very fit or very young. Did Walmart even carry "britches" I wondered? Then I prayed that they would, plain, cotton, and ample-sized.

A long time ago, a wise man taught me to leave the judging of this sort of thing to God. So it never crossed my mind that the five dollars might be spent on cheap wine or donuts. Others more cynical might find me naïve, so be it. What I do know is that pantries often have second-hand clothing or shoes for people down on their luck, but it is rare to find underwear.

A year or so later, it's still hard to admit, even to myself, that I froze after giving her the money. I turned away and never took the next step. The image of the old woman huddled on the bench, waiting in the cold rendered me useless. Maybe it was her asking for underpants, woman-to-woman that got to me. Maybe it was the otherworldliness of the entire situation. I had never heard anyone use the term "britches," although I remembered the word from novels. Or perhaps the real reason was grasping that this could be me.

I failed the old woman wanting "britches" by giving her five dollars and walking away. We didn't share first names, discuss the wintery weather or shop together as women do. She went her way and I went mine, a routine business exchange so it seemed. I was the one; however, who got a rare gift from this encounter. The image of the old woman haunted me, making me wonder. In this season of Advent, was she there truly waiting in need or simply giving me, a sinner, a chance to be Christ-like?

A surprise Christmas check from Good Shepherd Episcopal Church and the generosity of two parishioners made redemption possible. Blessings upon the old woman, I knew exactly what to do. We loaded up my truck with underwear: men's briefs in various colors and sizes and a selection of women's panties. Then we hit the streets, stopping at spots where homeless people gather. We greeted each other and exchanged pleasantries. Then, everyone got a pair of "britches" along with a piece of decency they deserved. Hallelujah!

GUILT IS GOOD

It was a freeze night in Austin. Shawn in short sleeves sought me out looking for a coat. Going from volunteer to volunteer, I was unsuccessful in my search and the evening events proceeded as usual. Shawn was one of seventy or so men who departed from the ARCH, Austin Resource Center for the Homeless, on city buses and were dropped at St. Ignatius Martyr to spend the night. They marked their sleeping spots on the floor with a blanket or bag and got in line for a meal prepared by gracious church volunteers. This Catholic Church is one of seven sites in the city that shelters homeless men when it is 32 degrees or 35 and wet. These men were grateful for the welcome and warm safe place to rest. Many were asleep by seven; lights were out at nine.

Up the next day at four, young Shawn tracked me down again. He was one you could not ignore for his razor-thin body was resplendent in tattoos, with little white space left on his canvas. His appearance was disarming. Shawn looked like an inter-terrestrial visitor mostly due to his facial "art." Above each eye, from lid to high forehead, a series of large brilliant blue/green exclamation points drew the observer in and created the impression that this man was in a constant state of awe or alarm.

Still with no jacket to be found, we talked. Shawn was open and honest. Recently released from prison, this time for "aggravated assault with a deadly weapon," he began to tell me how his life had changed after this third crime and punishment. He said he no longer "did drugs or alcohol, was not going to fight unless he had to protect himself, and in jail found Jesus." When asked what he wanted to do with his life, all of his "tats" seemed to light up. Shawn explained he wanted to design tattoos, not be the shop owner, rather the artist who created the designs. I respected his goal, which was a bit unusual since I do not even have pierced ears and have to brace myself when getting a flu shot. Yet here was this man celebrating the thousands of ink-filled needles that pierced his skin all for the sake of art— extraordinary!

After breakfast, one of the volunteers took off his sweater and gave it to short-sleeved Shawn. I added my scarf, and then surprise of all surprises, a fellow guest came up and said, "Where is that man who needs a coat?" and handed me a jacket. Suddenly guilt, garments, and grace seemed tangled, making givers and receivers indistinguishable—small miracles.

Buses began loading and volunteers busied themselves cleaning tables and stacking chairs. I was on trash detail and while on duty, left my little white plastic bag on a table by the door. It was filled with personal things I bring for the night: glasses, a flashlight, and toiletries. Shawn was the last to leave and I noticed my bag was missing. Instantly I knew what had happened and was saddened.

Off to work, I immersed myself in the tasks of the day; however, was still bothered by the breach of trust. Miraculously, faith in my fellow man was restored. A call from the church relayed that a man at the ARCH turned in a small white plastic bag to the guards and said, "I took something I should not have." Hallelujah! Repentance is possible for all of us! Shawn could have thrown the bag in the trash when he discovered what it contained, or lied that he found it, but most likely saw the copy of my driver's license, recalled our conversations, and his newly minted moral code could not be stifled.

Guilt can be good, not paralyzing guilt, but prodding guilt that shores up our better selves. Spirit-filled people of all faiths with good guilt stirring in their souls often ask for mercy, praying, "God, forgive me for what I have done and for what I have failed to do."

Good guilt, and an old woman listening to a young man's dreams— with God's blessing, isn't it amazing what can become of it for everyone!

GRACE-FILLED MOMENTS

Isn't it uncanny how some people can connect the dots from art to life, and if we are fortunate, we can follow their lead and in so doing, add layers of meaning to our lives? Austin's own Dave Steakley, Producing Artistic Director of Zach Theatre, is one such gifted "connector." In Zach's most recent production, *Grapes of Wrath*, based on the novel by John Steinbeck, Steakley directed a memorable opus full of pain and promise. It was, however, Steakley's approach to this play and to his actors and audience that set him apart from other artists. For him, *Grapes of Wrath* was not a period piece; rather, it was a flesh and bone reminder of the struggles homeless people of our city face.

By word of mouth, Steakley found me, a link to the homeless. His vision was that by some interaction between those who live on our streets and his actors, the experience might inform the actors' performance and, in turn, let the actors serve the homeless in some small way. Risky, revolutionary thinking, you bet, but Steakley knew art's purpose is grander than a round of applause. Baby steps were taken.

A few actors spent time in Wooldridge Park, shyly serving donuts and milk to people who make the park their home by day and sleep in hidden places in the city by night. Others served a turn in a soup kitchen or shelter for the homeless. These were not spotlight performances, just pocket-sized gestures of caring, one human being to another, and an opening up of possibilities.

I have lived on the streets with homeless people many times, but this Steakley-led experience was like no other, for this time I was facilitator as well as participant, and had the advantage of seeing diverse groups gently collide. In this atypical connection, two grace-filled moments gripped me.

One occurred on a Saturday morning as an actor from the Zach Company and I were leaving the University United Methodist Church. We had just spent part of the morning visiting with friends at the free breakfast and later sorting donations in the Fig Leaf, a clothing pantry. Amid our goodbyes in the parking lot, out of the corner of my eye I noticed a homeless man with a tray in his hand gently feeding a young, frail and totally handicapped man in a wheelchair.

I turned to my new friend from the world of the theatre and said, "Look, that says it all." Suddenly, the smells, the vacant stares, and the heartaches of the world we were visiting evaporated. When this happens, it is best not to analyze, question or pursue, just drink in the goodness and the beauty of the moment and hope it will make you into a better person than you have any right to be.

The second grace-filled moment occurred in the darkened Zach Theatre during the last scene of *Grapes of Wrath*, as I sat surrounded by homeless friends and recently homeless friends who now live in a safe house or RV. Together we witnessed the overwhelming selflessness of a young mother who has just lost her newborn and yet is willing to nurse a dying man.

The current of unspoken brotherhood zapped from stage to audience to each one of us and back.

We humans are a curious breed. We go to church hoping for revelation, and then let the river of everyday life wash over us until we are nearly numb. Now, church is a good thing, but it is not enough. It is never enough.

It is the grace-filled moments in our lives that can truly inspire and change us. Grace-filled moments don't come at our bidding; they are gifts in the truest sense and seem to me, the surest proof of the existence of God. While we don't summon up these moments, we have to be ready to host them.

Steakley envisioned a coupling of art and life, of past and present, and of haves and have-nots in directing *Grapes of Wrath*, I wonder, did he or any of us ever dream of the grace-filled moments that might follow?

GETTING OUT OF THE FUNK

We've all been there—feeling out of sorts, empty, and sometimes even downright gloomy. It can be a reaction to an everyday event, the flu, a fender-bender, a relationship gone sour or it can sneak up and clobber us when we least suspect it. Being in a funk is different than being anxious or depressed. Full blown anxieties and depression are more intense and long-lived, and often require professional help. Being in a funk is just a nasty part of being human. So how do we deal with it?

The suggestions are endless and come from everywhere, most of which I don't want to hear when I'm in the midst of a deep funk! The medical profession would probably recommend a check-up to rule out health conditions and question sleep and diet regimes. Body-conscious folks would propose physical exercise. Psychologists would suggest confiding in a friend, watching a comedy show, or listening to lively music. And advertisements would tempt me with retail therapy where shopping or rocky road ice cream cures all ills.

Okay, sometimes these things work, but not always. A funk is a funk is a funk, so I explored another approach.

Some people, I noticed, seem remarkably content and rarely rattled by outside forces; it appears that they learned to manage the funks by getting out of themselves. These centered and unflappable folks are unusually kind and display a generosity of spirit. They can be any age, and come from all walks of life with little or lots of financial resources. Essentially, they just do things consistently that lift others up, which in turn lifts them up, allowing for limited funk creep. Several Austin funk-fighting samurais come to mind.

Lawrence, a handicapped artist, has to crawl or use a wheel chair to get about. He supports himself by selling his paintings and often has barely enough to buy a sandwich. His funk indicator should be sky high, but Lawrence has found a way to cope. He thinks of others and then acts. Recently, he was given a bucket of chicken wings; one would imagine with empty pockets that he would gobble them up or hoard them. Not Lawrence. I watched him eat a few and then heave himself into his wheel chair in search of a young woman whom he knew was hungry and in need of a friend.

Lucy, a Holocaust survivor, has faced things most of us cannot imagine, yet her smile is ever-present and she is refreshingly upbeat. One of her secret funk weapons is organizing "Lucy's Un-stoppable Women's Gatherings." The women she handpicks, like me, feel honored to be part of a diverse group. We arrive, pot-luck in hand, ready to follow her lead. Lucy's rules are simple: "When speaking in the circle, talk about something that involves or excites you. Work, relationships, children, and grandchildren tales are forbidden." What Lucy forces us to do is to think positively about our own lives and find inspiration in each other.

Then there is Darrell, a high-tech executive, who did what most of us would consider unthinkable. He donated a kidney to his ex-wife. With humility and no bitterness, he said, "She is the mother of my children." Going through the mental anguish and physical pain of donating a kidney makes me shudder; however, most of us would probably do it for a child or a sibling, but to an ex-spouse, it's hard to imagine! Darrell surpassed the expected behavior of someone divorced and morphed into one whose generosity will keep him funk free for some time.

Interestingly, these friends of mine have diverse church-going experience. Lawrence is a Bible-toting, hymn-singing guy who often attends church under the bridge. Lucy with a traditional Jewish heart celebrates the holidays at home and at temple. And Darrell is a member of a mega evangelical church.

Believing in something bigger than oneself, being grateful and spiritually grounded in a faith practice, and then reaching out to others in consistent and sometimes dramatic ways seems the secret of fighting the funk.

Without preaching, just by example alone, these funk-bashers showed me a better way to live in the New Year.

FREDDIE

Friday evening I stopped for a light at the South Lamar Boulevard and U.S. 290 merge, that mixing bowl of multilayered ramps that demands defensive driving skills and Zen-like calm, and rolled down my window to greet a man "flying a sign." "No money" I said, "Just visiting." He was surprisingly delighted with my friendliness and old-fashioned word, "visiting." I asked his name, "Freddie Arbuckle Jr." he answered with dignity and pride. I told him mine. Money didn't matter to Freddie, but other pressing matters did, he said "I am so lonely; I have no one to talk to." "Well you have me now," I said.

Freddie had done some day labor earlier and was heading home to his tent in the woods. Feeling unrushed, we talked; the traffic light must have been jammed or perhaps time was suspended just for us. I told him I was on my way to the Mobile Loaves & Fishes Commissary to go out on the food truck and asked if he was hungry, suggesting that perhaps we could swing by his spot. He said, "Thanks, I don't need any food."

Keeping my right hand on the steering wheel, I extended my left hand to Freddie. Unlike most handshakes, we didn't pull apart, but hung on to each other the entire time we talked, feeling very much at home, hand-in-hand.

As I looked down at my hand enclosed in his, I saw our diverse worlds collide and connect; the white skin of my ancestors contrasting with the darker tones of his heritage. His hand was nearly square, dirt-spattered, and hard with calluses from honest labor and homelessness. My slender hand with old lady liver spots and blue veins visible through the thin skin felt insubstantial in his grasp, yet we fit together perfectly it seemed to both of us.

After awhile, the light turned green and I was on my way, but Freddie stayed in my thoughts. When I got home hours later, for no reason that I can fathom, I wrote down his name. That Sunday I did something unexpected, I read the death notices. It jumped out at me, "Freddie Arbuckle Jr., age 45 died, Friday night." I realized that I might have been the last person to talk to him.

Shocked, I tried to sort out what had happened to him and between us. I am conservative and a planner by nature. Bills are paid on time, oil changes and dental checks are on the calendar months ahead. I like being in control; however, sometimes I surprise myself by being impulsive. It's almost as if something takes over my senses temporarily and I act. This is what I believe happened when I rolled down my window and said, "No money, just visiting."

For most of my life, I attributed this kind of experience to spontaneity on my part often resulting in a serendipitous event, like all of the planets being aligned to produce an unforgettable moment where I was the beneficiary.

I no longer believe in serendipity; too many astonishing moments like connecting with Freddie hours before he died make me believe that there is a plan and a divine planner. For me, there is just no other explanation, otherwise, why did two strangers come together, hold hands, and share deepest feeling for a few moments on the side of a busy highway?

I believe in free will, but I don't believe that Freddie or I willed this incredible, intimate exchange. It happened miraculously outside of our doing.

Blessed by this encounter, I wonder if I can stop trying to control life and lean more frequently into the mystery that is full of grace? I wonder if I can say "Yes" to what I call the Holy Spirit and not know where it will take me?

Freddie spoke bravely of the fundamental fear we all have of being alone and unloved. But by his vulnerability and outreach to another person, I believe Freddie died full of love, from God, the Divine Planner who is love itself, through me, to him, and back again in a circle you could almost touch.

Freddie died of a heroin overdose that night.

HE'S FLYING WITH ME

"He's flying with me this time! You know how I can always tell."

This is how Malcolm began his phone call to me. What a conversation starter. I assume he was referring to God as his co-pilot. Smiling as I heard this remark, I could tell that Malcolm was feeling positive about himself and the world in general.

His life has been a series of major ups and downs, but in his 50s, he can still roust himself from life-threatening depression and keep on trucking. Forgotten by his family, fragile from muscular sclerosis, fighting addiction, frustrated as a failed musician, and scammed by "friends," Malcolm's road is never smooth. Yet he has a style and a generosity of spirit I admire. A Rod Stewart look-alike and wannabe,

Malcolm keeps his hair flowing and wild. Whenever he has a few extra bucks, he buys hair products to stay blond. He swears he is a great colorist and has offered to bleach my hair, but friendship only goes so far. His hearing, possibly related to MS or eardrum splitting jam sessions, is poor, so he spends a lot of time asking "What?" which can drive some people crazy. He has not a tooth in his mouth; however, he intends to get a full set of dentures when and if he can afford them and fit it into his schedule. This has been his plan for what seems like forever.

Despite his physical and sometimes mental challenges, this man is a consummate caretaker.

His greatest pleasure is noticing what others need and stepping in to help. He's the one who sweeps floors and stacks chairs in the shelter without being asked. He's the friend who shares his meager supply of tobacco with folks who need it more than he does. And he's the one who shows others how to negotiate the bus system, guiding strangers through complicated numbers, routes, and schedules.

This is the peaceable Malcolm, the Malcolm I love to hug, the Malcolm under control. But this side of my friend also can be lost during a pessimistic, reactionary, fault-finding period. When he is in one of these cycles, the world appears hostile to him and he can spin mildly out of control as a result. We have battled some of these bleak times together.

Since I have known him, he's been homeless, crashed in a flophouse, lived in a shelter, occupied a nice apartment, returned to the streets, and ended up in a shelter again with hopes for a slot in a rehabbed motel. At his lowest point, well actually our lowest point, Malcolm had to battle bed bugs in his apartment.

Despite being totally grossed out, we both got the exterminating techniques down pat.

During this crisis time when he was dealing with invasive insects, failing to pay rent, losing money, being evicted, fighting with social workers and landlords, and receiving a subpoena to appear in court, Malcolm was mad at the world. We were both nearly at our wits end. He felt and acted like a victim, and not a "sit in the corner and mope" kind of victim. He was a loud, accusatory, and alienating kind of victim.

Out of the blue and desperate, I said, "Malcolm, stop dealing with things this way and operate from your center of goodness." Shocked at this unusual statement, we both paused and wondered what it meant. The notion and the phrasing were foreign and not mine, clearly a gift from God.

Suddenly the clouds cleared and we both got it. Contrary to his bravado and boisterous behavior when besieged by troubles, Malcolm never believed he had any control or an ounce of goodness in him. He felt ugly and therefore acted ugly. A simple reminder to "operate from your center of goodness" changed everything. We have repeated it often to each other trying to solve problems in a new way.

All of us are created in the image of God. As His creatures, we are inherently good. How could we forget this?

DIGNITY

It was a summer day in Texas—103 sweltering degrees! I filled the trunk of my car with bottled water and ice. Not bagged ice from the supermarkets, but ice from the machines in neighborhoods where there is usually no air conditioning. Here for two dollars you can fill up a good-sized tub.

I headed to a back alley I knew where people find shelter in cardboard boxes or under plastic sheeting hung from a chain-link fence. As I approached an empty lot off the alley there was only one man standing in the blazing sun. The rest of the alley residents must have found shade somewhere else. My formerly homeless friend, who helped me load up the ice, preferred to stay in the car. She was street-smart and always had 911 ready to press on her phone.

So I walked by myself toward the lone man who upon seeing me cried out in a loud voice over and over again, "I need you, I need you!" With the accompanying pelvic thrusts, I had no doubt what he meant. When we got near each other, he grasped my upper arms and continued his shouting and thrusting. By the grace of God, thoughts and words not of my doing appeared. I looked him squarely in the eye and said calmly, "You do not want to do this. It will rob you of your dignity." Almost immediately he stopped shouting and thrusting, cast his eyes downward, turned around, and started to walk away.

I called to him, "Wait, I have ice and water for you." He stopped, startled by my words it seemed. Reaching out, I handed him water and ice in a cup. He didn't speak and neither did I. Everything was already spoken.

When I got back into the car, my friend said." What was that all about?" I said, "I really don't know. I am fine, yet I can still feel the red-hot heat and that man's fingers pressing into my upper arms." It was an out-of-body experience—a strangely illuminating time—like the man and I were the only two people on the face of the scorched earth. The air was still yet suffused with a gentle loving presence. I saw that man as he really was and he must have seen me the same way. Amid the desolation, the drink and the drugs in this alley, there is hope. A hand-painted sign on a house that backs up to the alley reads, "God lives in this place." I think He must.

Rabbi David Rosen writes, "Above all, all obligations towards our fellow human beings (and indeed towards ourselves) are rooted in the Biblical teaching that the human person is created in the Divine Image and thus with the sacred right to life, freedom and dignity."

Remembering the words that spontaneously flowed from my mouth to the desperate man, I got to thinking. When we dismiss the dignity of the human person a downward spiral begins for each one of us and for our communities large and small. Either by ignorance or arrogance this disregard soon affects every aspect of our lives.

He/she, we/they thoughts flood our minds and our emotions and we act impulsively and cruelly against others as if it were our right to do so. We tolerate slurs and verbal attacks on people as normal conduct and turn a blind eye even when we feel the tug in our hearts knowing these behaviors are wrong. We secretly or openly cheer for those who divide, rather than support those who unite.

Maybe our earthly task is to honor each other's inherent dignity and help each other reflect this gift however challenging it may be. Perhaps it's best to start small—reaching out to one person with love and without fear—and then another, and another.

The man in the empty lot was right in his crying loudly, "I need you, I need you!" Putting aside his sexual demands, he spoke the essential truth. We do need each other desperately to function, to live a dignified life full of meaning and gratitude.

The fundamental question is always present—how do we choose to live?

LOVE

God loves us, that's all. It's that simple, not a
complicated agenda, just pure love handed out
freely to each one of us.

BEING LOVED

What is it we all want most? Is it money, fame, power? Is it a job, good health, a home? Is it relief from mental and physical pain? Is it an opportunity to get an education? Is it to enjoy the freedoms guaranteed to Americans in The Bill of Rights, an amendment to the United States Constitution, including Freedom of Religion, Speech, and the Press?

Certainly a few of these matter only a little, while others matter a lot. To me the answer is simpler. I think what all of us want is to be loved unconditionally. But what does this mean and how do we know we are loved?

Those who read the Bible and perhaps go to church or temple, believe that they are each cherished by a loving God. It is the foundation of their faith. Many who don't believe in a creator God, still admire the wonders of our world and our lives. Sometimes seeing a baby come into the world from the physical act of sperm and egg connecting is enough to inspire belief in a loving superpower.

Yet even for those Bible-reading and church-going folks, doubt creeps in. Who is this God who supposedly loves me despite my many shortcomings? The *leap of faith* is enormous and not always satisfying in its specificity, which I guess is why it's called a *leap of faith*. Being awkward, earth-bound, pleasure-seeking creatures, we don't often feel worthy of love. We can't even imagine what being loved without limits looks like or feels like.

So this is where dogs come in. It could be a heresy for the church hierarchy; however, here goes my canine theory. Working dogs and dogs in our families, or even in a shelter, love us unconditionally. They have the capacity to forgive, forget, and love us again and again, even after we fail them. They soften our hearts and show us how to love, not just by our words, but by our actions. They give us a glimpse of God's unconditional love, which we cannot really fathom.

With a pack mentality, dogs relish relationships. Children grasp this intuitively. People who are lonely, handicapped, or suffering often turn to dogs for comfort—instant canine therapy. Dogs don't care if you are old, or didn't get the promotion, or flunked the math test. When you return home from a 20-minute errand or a day away, they greet you as if you were the most important person on the planet. It's love you can feel.

Children and most adults think of their dogs as family members. Children, especially, are suspicious of heaven if their dogs cannot enter. There has been much theological debate on this topic from scores of people—everyone from Aristotle to The Reverend Billy Graham. As you can imagine, opinions vary. Today, the most we can hope for is to hang onto a line from the prayer at the end of **LAUDATO SI',** an ENCYCLICAL LETTER OF THE HOLY FATHER FRANCIS, May 2015: "For all the creatures of this earth, for not one of them is forgotten in your sight." Fingers crossed! Pups in heaven.

Jackie, a pound rescue pooch, is the life-line of love for my friend who lives alone in a housing project, and Jackie gets her favorite barking bacon strips as often as her mistress can manage. Rascal, a mini wolf-dog, lives on the streets with his master, a metal-studded man who sees that Rascal wears his coat when it is cold and sleeps next to him at night to ward off the wind. When I first encountered homeless people with dogs, I was judgmental thinking—"How can they pay for dog food and the vet? Isn't that poor money management?" Over time I learned, the dogs were key to their survival. Their dogs were the tangible, unconditional love, homeless people—all people crave.

So to my way of thinking, dogs are sort of like four-legged ambassadors or maybe better, missionaries of love, showing us here and now what it means to be loved without conditions or limits. Not for what we have, or do, or look like, but for who we are inside.

Perfectly made.

By God.

HOLY

I've been weeding out books and boxing them up for Goodwill; still I have three bulging shelves of spiritual books. I relish new titles, savor old favorites, and dabble in prayer and poetry books. Basically, I just like having them around. They're a comfort in this busy world of technology that's always changing and expecting me to change as well.

I display seasonal books on a little shelf in my library nook that I hope will shout, "Open me, see what is inside to help you grow spiritually." Some authors never disappoint: C.S. Lewis, Rumi, Richard Rohr, Henri Nouwen, and Thomas Merton.

For some time, I have been taken by the *The Best American Spiritual Writings*, a collection that is published yearly. These selections appeared in other publications and are included for their unique voice and worthiness. The range of topics is impressive.

Admittedly, I am a sucker for books with lists or just one thing on a page, anything—a quote, a prayer, or a suggestion that might jump start my spiritual life. *Prayers for Peace, Power Lines: Celtic Prayers about Work, Always We Begin Again: The Benedictine Way of Living* satisfy.

Big coffee table books like *The Amazing Faith of Texas* or little books like *The Pocket Pema Chodron* attract me in differing ways; big ones invite browsing, while little ones tuck conveniently in a purse for downtime away from home.

Inspirational stories of faith stay with me long after I reach the end. Immaculee Ilibagiza's *Left to Tell, Discovering God Amidst the Rwandan Holocaust* and Viktor E. Frankl's *Man's Search for Meaning* are two books that come to mind that have the power to change hearts and minds.

A half century ago, I attended a Catholic College where there were rigorous theology requirements for all students. Together we plowed through the tissue-paper-thin pages of St. Thomas Aquinas' *Summa Theologica* and tried to understand the questions posed and the answers given in these voluminous tomes. Not easy for anyone, especially 18 and 19 year olds who were more interested in dates and dances. Add on St. Augustine's *City of God* and other dense and lengthy works that were required reading and one would think that I would have a literary spiritual structure that is sturdy. It is, but those early readings even in their brilliance and complexity are never enough. Over time shoring up must be done to keep a spiritual house from crumbling.

My shelf of books is a resource especially during this Lenten Season, where my resolve for forty days is to add something to daily life, not subtract, as is often the custom. Consistently reading something to feed my soul will replace giving up wine or chocolate.

Person-to-person encounters, however, are often the turning points in my faith journey, and they pop up where I least expect them. A Valentine's Day happening recently topped any reading I'd been doing. Each year I put socks, candy, and a valentine in a party bag and take them to homeless people on the streets. After delivering bags to a crowd, a man came up to me and said, "Pardon me, thank you for this kindness. Are you a church-going woman?" I replied, "Well I try to be a faith-filled person." "Me too," he said. "I like to read the Bible and I know what 'Bible' means, but lately I've wondered, what the word 'Holy' on the front of my Bible, means?" From the broad smile on his face, I sensed he already had the answer. He said, "I was told in a dream, HOLY stands for HE ONLY LOVES YOU." The revelation apparently woke him and he laughed out loud with delight to discover this. He then explained, "It does not mean HE ONLY LOVES YOU with the accent on YOU. It means HE ONLY LOVES YOU, with the accent on ONLY LOVES." In other words, God loves us, that's all. It's that simple, not a complicated agenda, just pure love handed out freely to each one of us.

I got in my car and wrote down this nugget from a wise and joy-filled scholar-in-residence on the streets.

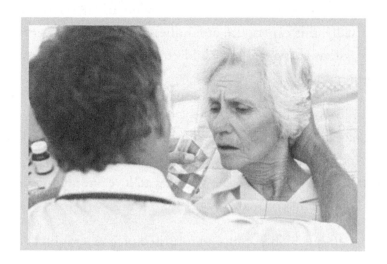

HOLY FAMILIES

An angel visits a virgin to tell her that she is going to bear a son. This teenager is betrothed to an older man with whom she has not had relations. According to the custom of the day, if a woman was found to be with child before marriage she could be abandoned or stoned to death. Her intended husband at first considers divorcing her, then in a dream is told, "Do not be afraid to take Mary your wife into your home." Matthew 1:20. He listens, doesn't walk away, and becomes a foster dad.

This was the first Holy Family—Mary, Joseph, and the son of God—Jesus.

Although we know little of this Holy Family's early life, we imagine Mary and Joseph did what most new parents do: they fed their infant son, sang him lullabies, and rocked him to sleep. Warned of a death threat for all male babies, they carried him to safety fleeing by night to escape the massacre, likely being homeless during their flight. Sadly, this experience of families on the run, refugees fleeing for life, often carrying their children on perilous journeys, is still happening today.

The family is the human cell of society. Any love that exists is born out of family life and the ripples affect individuals, neighbors, towns, cities, and nations, which may be one reason why God chose his son to be born into a family, to show us how to love one another in times of joy and in times of trial.

Like the unique Holy Family—a surprised pregnant virgin betrothed to an older man—there is no one design that makes a family.

Wanda, an energetic grandmother, lives in a tiny, ready-to-teardown rental unit with her son, his wife, their two children, and her pregnant daughter. They squeeze into this crumbling space without complaining. Each morning Wanda drives her grandson to a magnet school across town so he will have the opportunity to attend a school of excellence, then she heads off to her minimum-wage job. At the end of the day, she retraces her steps still smiling.

Gustavo, a house painter, is a hard worker as is his wife. They have a teen-aged son and a young daughter. They manage their money carefully so that each December they can return to Mexico for nine days to celebrate *Las Posadas*, a reenactment of the nativity with processions and prayers culminating with their extended family and neighbors enjoying a Christmas meal together. They relish their roots and want to pass on traditions.

Ana works six long days in a nail salon, then goes home to prepare dinner for her husband, three school-aged children, and her father who lives with them. Recently they have taken in her husband's two adult brothers who are immigrants from Vietnam. This has meant shifting sleeping arrangements in the small house and adding two more mouths to feed, but Ana says, "This is what families do; this is what others did for me when I came to America."

Charles, a middle-aged professional, lives with his mother who has Alzheimer's disease. He feels fortunate to be with her. Helped by a circle of loving caregivers, he wants to ensure that his mother's declining years are as pleasant as can be. She is almost completely nonverbal, but has not lost her wonder for the world in the whirl of the ceiling fan or the softness of a tissue.

These holy families, and there are so many more, do not even know that they are holy. They just operate from their center of goodness binding the wounds of our fragile world with love. They understand that this is simply what we are called to do, to care for each other, to love one another, although the doing is endless and not always easy. There are hands to hold and hearts to heal. There are babies to bathe and bodies to bury. There are times to savor and tears to shed.

The Feast of the Holy Family, which is on the Sunday following Christmas, is perhaps a good time to whisper a prayer of thanksgiving for all families whose holy work makes our world a better place.

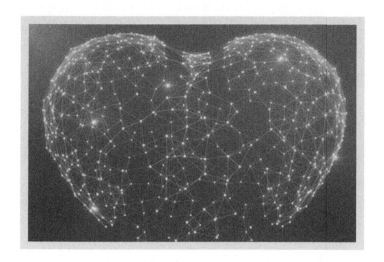

A VALENTINE ADJUSTMENT

On Saturday afternoon, I gently rock my four-month-old grandson and together we watch his two-year-old sister build a castle with blocks. Time stands still as I absorb the sweet smell of baby, the downy fluff atop his head, and her precise attention to balancing block upon block. Love flows unbidden. I feel my heart open physically and am moved beyond words. Their start to life is extraordinary. Healthy, and knowing only a stable, safe environment, they are the center of their parents' universe. There is no limit to their potential as human beings. My valentine to them seems almost unnecessary and yet I send out imagined poems, and songs, and love notes as grandmothers do.

On Sunday night, I am with nearly 100 homeless men. It is a "Freeze Night" in Austin and St. Ignatius Martyr Catholic Church is one of the seven interdenominational faith communities that has volunteered to take in homeless people when there is no room in the shelters. It is 32 degrees. Metro buses pick the clients up at the Austin Resource Center for the Homeless and take them to the assigned church depending on the day of the week. St. Ignatius holds Sunday night holy for these men, as do I.

At six, they hurry through the doors of the Family Center, aptly named for these are our bothers in Christ. Some carry sleeping bags or blankets. Some tote suitcases or plastic bags, and some have nothing but the clothes on their back. At the door, we welcome them. Smiles and "thanks" are abundant while most scurry to secure a spot in the gym.

Anthony arrives in a wheelchair with his urinal hooked on the arm. He says bluntly; I can't always make it to the toilet. Jerry also arrives in a wheelchair and we search the room for a somewhat out-of-the-way spot for him. Both of these wheelchair-bound men are elderly. Pete, much younger yet physically challenged as well, brings his diabetic supplies in an insulated tote and looks for an outlet to run his breathing machine.

Gracious church parishioners prepare a meal: chili dogs, salad, fruit, and cookies. A do-it-yourself beverage bar with instant coffee and hot chocolate helps ward of the chill. Remarkably, there is no pushing, shoving or un-gentlemanly behavior in line. They are grateful for any kindness offered.

After dinner, many of the men are already bedded down, wrapped in a blanket or stretched out on the bare floor. A talented church musician entertains with mandolin, guitar, and recorder until we turn off the lights at nine, what a gift for these men who probably can't recall a lullaby. As the bulk of the men drift off, I overhear one say, "Lord, let me live another day." A quiet amen chorus echoes his prayer.

Several times a night, I walk among them, tucking a stray blanket, handing out a cough drop, and smiling at the one or two guests sitting at a table unable to sleep. Random cell phones ring, the bathroom door slams again and again, cries from bad dreams punctuate the silence, and snoring reaches decibels I never imagined.

For many people, including me at times, these men are the un-washed and some would say, "the un-lovely in our world." They represent all of the other "un-s" we label so heartlessly: the un-promising, the un-cultured, the un-well, the un-connected, the un-cooperative, the un-acceptable.

On Saturday afternoon with my grandbabies, when love flows spontaneously from the sheer sensation of being with them, drinking in their purity and promise, everything seems so simple and of my doing. In my smugness, I forget to pray.

On Sunday night with the homeless men, blessedly the contrast prompts me to say my daily prayer, "Lord, help me reflect your love to all those I meet." Once uttered, I am amazed at the feeling of love un-leashed. Unfamiliar smells, bothersome sounds, and lives gone awry fade in the background. The homeless men become a valentine like no other I've ever sent or received. Prayer clearly opens the heart and I remember, "We love because he first loved us." 1 John 4:19

GIFT GIVING

Crane-like, he stands on a small asphalt island amid a turbulent sea of man-made machines. A reed-thin leg is cradled between rag-wrapped wooden crutches. His head like some great marsh bird is bent low. Could this anomaly be from the same accident or illness that took his leg or is this posture the result of millions of small carefully planned steps, peering at the ground to gauge where to place his foot?

Of indeterminate age, this white man has leathery brown skin and red-rimmed eyes. His hands are dirt speckled and calloused from constant crutch use. Un-barbered grey curls escape from a cap. He turns his head to the side to see, as he must. Then his eyes open wide, a smile slowly spreads across his face and he says, "And how are you?"

Our exchanges are brief, all conversations controlled by traffic lights and non-stop transit, but despite these limitations, I know that Jesse's world is contained within one mile. Even when it is freezing, he will not venture outside this safe circle to go to a shelter in the city.

Most days you can find him on his small asphalt island. He is a flier, (a homeless person who holds up a sign asking for help) but flies no sign, his need is apparent. At dusk, in rush-hour madness, he risks life and limb making his way home. It is a larger island under the freeway that once was zeroscaped with large rocks. Now from lack of care it is overgrown with native saplings and wild brush. Jesse is completely camouflaged in this strange urban forest. His safety is further ensured by a moat of roads surrounding his island.

The International Crane Foundation states that, "Humans are the most dangerous predators of cranes." And most likely the biggest threat for this crane-like man.

It is the Christmas season and although not kingly, I aspire to be a gift-bearer with the perfect present. Seeing Jesse I say, "What do you need?" He points down and says, "A new pair of shoes, size eight and a half." On a mission, I head to the store and buy a pair of sturdy boots with thick soles to keep out the cold and provide stability.

When I return with the boots, Jesse says, "These are too small, I am a size ten and a half and prefer sneakers." Interestingly enough both of us refer to his needing a pair of shoes as if we have to pay homage to his phantom leg.

Back to the store I go to return the boots and purchase a perfect pair of sneakers in the right size. They smack of quality and style: saddle-brown with neon orange trim and matching orange laces. These seem ideal for a man with one leg who travels across highways at a snail's pace dodging speeding vehicles. Maybe the Day-Glo orange will make him more visible. A pair of red, orange, and yellow flame patterned socks I tuck into the sneakers to complete the look.

Several days later I see him and he is wearing his old sneakers, I ask, "Where are the new ones?" He says, "They are too flashy for me; I am a plain man." So I take back the snazzy socks, make another trip to the store and get black socks, brown laces, and a permanent black marker to cover up the orange trim.

Ultimately, he remains in his old sneakers and says to me, "Why don't you return the new ones?" I suggest re-gifting to a friend in need which makes us both happy.

The Feast of the Epiphany, sometimes called Twelfth Night, is usually celebrated on January 6. It recalls Matthew's Gospel that wise men from the east followed a star to Bethlehem where they found the infant king and offered him gifts of gold, frankincense, and myrrh. What became of these gifts? Was some of the gold used for necessities and the rest given to the poor? Were the rare perfumes re-gifted with grace like Jesse's shoes? Despite theories we don't know.

Crane-like, Christ-like this plain man patiently waits just to be noticed, to be loved. That's all.

Epiphany.

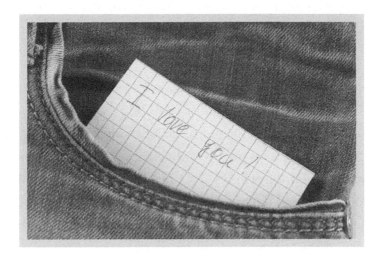

I LOVE YOU

I thought I knew him, the burly man sitting on the bench at the bus stop, so I made a quick turn into the convenience store behind him. My car was recently stocked with amazing hand-knit blankets tucked into homemade carry totes—perfect for those living on the streets—light weight and warm. A faith-filled friend said, she prays as she knits for the person who will be receiving the blanket. Double blessing!

I hurried to my suspected friend with a carry tote in hand and walked around to greet him. The shock of seeing him face-to-face nearly did me in—it was not the man I thought I knew, but a stranger with a frightful appearance. He had long hair and a long beard, both grisly and grey. His head, seemingly too large even for his large body, tilted to one side. One good eye scanned my presence. The other eye drew me in and repulsed me. It was recessed and red, wandering and wasted, surrounded by a mass of pus-filled mounds. His enormous nose spread from cheek to cheek, surely capable of sniffing out the smallest of scents. And his gaping mouth contained only one tooth—a top right incisor which was askew and menacing.

As I handed him the blanket, he gave me an other-worldly grin and said, "Thank you for your kindness." I didn't ask him his name or give him mine as I usually do. I didn't offer my hand or hug him as is my custom. I was simply overwhelmed by ugliness. Wanting to do some good on this wintery day didn't happen—just the opposite did. I found myself looking at this hideous homeless man on a bus stop bench and experiencing the phrase, "beauty is in the eye of the beholder." I saw no beauty and hated my reaction more than his ugliness.

Sometime later, a sliver of empathy… redemption really, emerged as I realize that this man was somebody's baby once, treasured perhaps, and not thought unbeautiful, unsightly, or unlovable.

The poem "Falling in Love" is attributed to Jesuit priest, Father Pedro Arrupe to celebrate Valentine's Day.

Nothing is more practical than
Finding God, that is, than
FALLING IN LOVE
in a quite absolute, final way.
What you are in love with,
what seizes your imagination,
will affect everything.
It will decide

what will get you out of bed
in the morning,
what you do with your evenings,
how you spend your weekends,
what you read, whom you know,
what breaks your heart,
and what amazes you with joy and gratitude.
Fall in love, stay in love,
and it will decide everything.

When I first read this poem, I envisioned it an eloquent ode to a lover, or a child, or a close-knit family. After several readings and time to digest the words between readings, I wondered, "Did I miss the real meaning? Was Father Aruppe encouraging us to go beyond what at first glance seemed a simple valentine—was he urging us to think broadly, deeply, boldly?" Is he saying, "Yes" to God, really falling in love, which will "affect everything?" And in so doing, will our lives be vastly different? Does loving our neighbor as is preached by many faiths, actually mean falling in love with each other, which will "decide everything?" Will petty squabbles with our families, colleagues, neighbors, and merchants abate if we fall in love with each other? Will terrorism and wars cease?

Love is essential in life yet its meaning is difficult to decipher. The ancient Greeks described various kinds of love, agape, unconditional selfless love as members of the family of man, being the hardest to digest and embody. Is this the ultimate test of our humanity—living a life for others, with others, loving each other with abandon—the beautiful ones who take our breath away just by looking at them, and the ugly ones who do the same? Can we do it—say "I love you" and mean it? To everyone?

As for me, I need to find that burly gentleman who said, "Thank you for your kindness," and shake his hand, surprise him with a hug, and say, "I love you."

WHAT IS IT THAT
OPENS OUR HEART?

Let's face it. For the most part it's all about me—my pleasure, my pain, my wants, my world. We are driven by self, security, and success. The true saints who care for children and for ill or aging family members with devotion have moved out of the ego circle by accepting their role. Their hearts are opened even when flooded by fatigue or frustration.

For the rest of us, including those whose hearts seem to have turned to stone, tiny cracks can appear that let light in and change who we are. I had the opportunity to see this transformation some years ago, and it was breathtakingly beautiful.

With a zany idea to host a spontaneous birthday party for the homeless folks who hang out in the alley between the Austin Resource Center for the Homeless (the ARCH) and the Salvation Army (the Sally), I set to work. Because I was head of a school, I had access to young artists, so I asked students in first through fifth grades to make a birthday card for someone they did not know. What an array of drawings and birthday wishes I received—balloons, hearts, rainbows, and sweet words: "I hope you have a good day;" "Happy, Happy, Birthday to a special friend;" and "You are loved." I put these better-than-Hallmark cards in a white wicker basket to distribute.

Birthday parties need more than cards, so I bought old-fashioned Dixie cups that come with little flat spoons and a scoop of vanilla ice cream, and birthday cupcakes. When I arrived at the entrance to the alley, my homeless friend met me. She took over the ice cream delivery from her wheel chair. My job was cupcakes. Balancing the bakery boxes carefully, I scanned the crowd looking for another helper. The perfect birthday party assistant appeared, asking, "May I help you?" He was joyful, high on life aided by some chemicals I suspect, but it didn't matter. Personifying the spirit of giving, he danced through the crowd with the wicker basket on his arm handing out birthday cards.

Within five minutes, there was an amazing change in the atmosphere of the alley. Here, where there is usually depression, anger, isolation, shouting, and sometimes fights, peace reigned.

As the folks began to sense the spontaneous goodness of a birthday party just for them and looked at their cards, conversation flowed. I overheard, "My birthday is in September, when is yours?" "Oh, let me see your card." "Look at this greeting to me!" A few even offered constructive criticism: "Birdday isn't spelled right" and "This child need more practice in penmanship," but the comments were laced with love.

This strange island of calm continued. Small waves of good will washed over everyone, and hearts of stone began to show cracks—light entering from ice cream and cupcakes, but mostly from children's unexpected caring hearts.

This is how God creates in us a new heart. We build hearts of stone, layer upon layer, believing we are forgotten, unworthy and unloved. Then we are cracked open in the most unforeseen ways. It is different for each one of us and astonishing every time it happens.

Miraculously, cracks continue to appear. Feeling awestruck when holding a newborn baby or animal that causes a lump in our throats, creates a crack. Seeing a spectacular sunset or hearing a haunting melody that catches us unaware and moved, creates a crack. Receiving an unexpected kindness when suffering that leaves us teary, creates a crack. And discovering that there's a surprise birthday party in an alley for you, a homeless person, creates a crack.

I will skip sending Valentine cards this year and just open my heart with layers and layers of love—to the tantruming toddler in the grocery line, to the old person in front of me fumbling for a bus pass, and to the gaggle of teens careening past me in the mall—to everyone in my path.

Real love unleashed.

"I will give you a new heart and put a new spirit within you; and I will remove the heart of stone from your flesh and give you a heart of flesh."
–Ezekiel 36: 26

REFLECTION:
LESSONS FROM THE STREETS

Lessons from the streets learned from years
of hanging out with homeless folks

GENEROSITY

This is noticeable in any group, in any culture, in any place. With homeless people, it is no different. So many times I witnessed people in a food line, as the supplies were dwindling, say, "Give it to him, motioning to the man behind him, I am not hungry." My friend Kim gave me a fuzzy warm blanket when I was on the streets and had none. She looked at my meager supply of stuff and said, "Without this, you won't last the night." She was right, and I carried it with me for three days and three nights.

ARTISTIC PASSIONS

They are there on the streets, just like in the suburbs and cities. Laura and Lawrence painted, Bear designed jewelry, Sam took photographs, and Susie did needlework. Supplies, a place to work, and maybe an occasional sale were the only worries.

CONNECTING

It's the essential thing for all of us. Once, I met a homeless man who was shivering and looking for a blanket in the frigid evening. He asked for my help. The shelters were closed. I did not know him, but said, "Come on, let's go to Walmart and buy a sleeping bag." We had a good time singing old rock and roll songs in the car on the way to the store. There he selected his bag, and his color and we headed back to the car and continued to sing, hymns, this time. Later, I dropped him off downtown. As he got out of my car, he said, "Judy, this was never about the sleeping bag." For years, I didn't understand what he meant. Now, I think I do.

HELPING

Wanting to be of help as humans, sets us apart from mere takers. I was in awe of the homeless people I knew who volunteered on a regular basis. Alan was a library aide. A normally angry and sullen old woman made the coffee every Saturday at the church brunch for homeless people in the city. Laura, could not have lunch with me on Saturdays, my free day, because she worked at The Fig Leaf, a clothing pantry. It's so easy to think that we with homes are the only givers with time and talent.

FAITH

It is what sustains us! Jim carried a medal of Mary on his empty key chain. Darrell, a Jew, was proud of his rosary. Homeless folks swarming around shelters let me bless them on Ash Wednesday. Some Catholics knew the meaning of the ashes I placed on their foreheads in the sign of a cross, and others, just wanted to believe in something or someone.

SURVIVAL

Homeless people have amazing coping skills. They have mastered complex bus routes, necessary for their basic transportation system and for staying warm in freezing weather and cool in heat waves. They know and share their knowledge of which churches serve food, and when. They can find open bathrooms—not easy! They use the internet for information and communicating. They find spots for sleeping in the city and the country that sometimes are safe.

PERSEVERANCE

Jonas, a gentle man who is often in and out of mental hospitals, says to me, "I will get a job."

IMPROVISING

Some of us rely on YouTube for how-to advice. Homeless people are way-ahead of us. They have to be. They figured out cardboard makes an okay mattress. They strap household goods on an old backpack with found rope. They take a hard-boiled egg, a packet of mayonnaise, and a roll from the food truck and make an egg salad sandwich before our eyes. They use their shoes or a bicycle tire for a pillow, welcoming sleep and keeping their valuables safe.

GRATITUDE

It isn't always in your face, but it's there. Wolf, who got back on his feet in another state, sent an email, "Thanks for feeding me all those years when I was living on the streets." Tom, came up to the Mobile Loaves & Fishes truck in the Walmart parking lot and gave me a ten dollar bill. He too said, "Thanks for feeding me when I couldn't feed myself."

FOOD

It is necessary of course, but it is only the first step. Listening, understanding, friendship, and support in a variety of areas must follow.

CONVERSATION

It's how we connect as humans. For homeless folks, it is not so different. We discuss the weather, where we're from, how our day is going. I am always trying to go gently into their world, being careful not to intrude. It's the same as meeting people anywhere, being cordial, open, and friendly is how to do it. Early one morning, at a shelter, an out-of-work carpenter spent time visiting with me. Suddenly, he touched his un-shaven face and apologized, saying, "Forgive me for looking like this, but I couldn't go inside to clean-up, this conversation be just too delicious!"

ENTERTAINMENT

Without houses, most homeless people find other ways to enjoy life. Fireworks, movies or concerts in the park, street fairs, church gatherings, libraries, friends, and street action—firetrucks, police chases, and arrests keep them busy.

HYGIENE

No home, no personal bathroom or laundry facilities means being grungy at times, but also finding ways to stay clean. Public bathrooms, (in limited supply) at least have a toilet and a sink. Public fountains can be bathtubs when the city is asleep. Laundromats help if you have the funds. Or, you can be like Bruce who says, "I wear disposable clothes."

SIMPLE PLEASURES

Chocolate, a smile, a bottle of water on a hot day, a brief exchange, "Hi, how is your day going?", a warm blanket in winter, a dry spot when it rains, new socks, good coffee.

SIGNS OF LOVE

Eye contact, a smile, a hand shake, a pat on the back, a high-five, sign language for the deaf community, a simple, "I love you," a hug if you are comfortable. For me from Jim, who seems to live in a world of demons, a gentle kiss on my cheek.

COMPASSION

Two homeless men visiting their friend in the hospital. A guest in a food line, saying, "Can I have a plate for my girlfriend who has MS?" A call to me from homeless friends, sitting on a street curb asking, "How is your bronchitis?"

ENDURANCE

Carrying your belongings on your back all day or stashing it somewhere hidden in hopes that it will be there when you return, wishing for one meal a day, sleeping in fits and starts, worrying about arrests and robberies, being on the streets with a cold, the flu, a sprained ankle, a wound, looking for a place to sit and rest your feet, bearing the distain of non-homeless people.

CONCLUSION

Throughout history certainly, but especially in our lifetime if we are honest, we grapple with the seemingly senseless, measureless pain of poor and homeless people. The *why* looms large. Consider, for a moment, that in the most elemental way, the most radical way, they exist for us. Not as our servants, but as our masters. Not as our dependents, but as our liberators. If we are mindful and open to their lives—our lives can change. It is possible that their pain can diminish our selfishness and in its place allow compassion to grow, their gift to us—becoming more human.

This insight is staggering in itself. Still, we are left with the question, "What am I to do to reach out to a homeless person? How am I to be my brothers' keeper?" A few suggestions:

- Smile at least to those on the streets or through the car

window

- Say "Hello" or "How is your day going?"

- Offer a bottle of water on a hot day

- Give socks anytime, always welcome

- Buy a drink or sandwich for the person on the sidewalk while entering a favorite coffee or lunch spot

- Befriend the neighborhood homeless persons on your street or your intersection, get their names, ask them what they need, remember them at holidays, find out their birthday so you can help them celebrate

- Have on hand a list of services for homeless people

- Support the mental health initiatives and recovery programs in your town

- Be aware of job banks

- Know of housing opportunities for homeless people or people who have limited income

- Learn about work being done by churches and other nonprofits to aid homeless people, help fund or volunteer

- Find out about hospitals and health support centers, especially wellness programs that reduce emergency room visits for homeless people

- Applaud and aid your city food bank and local pantries

- Think about the thousands of homeless people trying to find shelter during a thunderstorm, a snow storm, or an icy night

- Imagine having no money, no credit card, no family, few

friends—if any

- Begin to notice the homeless people around you each day

- Take one small step toward being your brother's keeper

- Pray for them and for all of us that we might respond with respect, care, and grace.

Each one of us belongs to this mighty family of man. We share the same home—planet earth. And, as in all families, our singular ones to our worldwide family, squabbles sometimes happen, meanness can surface, and violence too often erupts. In addition, we/they thoughts and actions consume us.

Kindness, which is love expressed, may be the only thing that can save us.

ACKNOWLEDGMENTS

I wish to thank a number of people and organizations for guiding me on this incredible journey. Alan Graham, founder of Mobile Loaves & Fishes and Community First, you were the spark, not only for the creation of these amazing support systems for homeless people in Austin, Texas, but also for designing the first Street Retreat in 2003, which I went on with you—both of us novices! After my numerous questions about our 72 hours to be spent on the streets, you taught me a valuable lesson, you said, "Judy, let it go." I did and I have continued to go confidently where the spirit guides.

Mobile Loaves & Fishes' food trucks volunteers hit the streets 7 nights a week, 365 days a year to serve the homeless, delivering food, clothing, and hygiene products and other life-sustaining items. With the support of more than 19,000 volunteers and more than 5 million meals served, Mobile Loaves & Fishes is the largest prepared feeding program to the homeless and working poor in Austin, Texas.

Community First! Village is a 27-acre master-planned community that provides affordable, permanent housing and a supportive community for the disabled, chronically homeless in Central Texas.

Thank you to St. John Neumann Catholic Church, my parish, for being the place of faith where Mobile Loaves & Fishes was birthed by a small group of men in 1998. So many fellow parishioners went on this first *Street Retreat* with Alan and me. We were the brave, the fearful, the ignorant, the blessed, cared for by our homeless brothers and sisters on the streets.

The University United Methodist Church deserves special recognition. I learned about your *Radical Hospitality* credo first from homeless street friends who slept in your parking lot, got clothes from your clothing pantry—The Fig Tree—and ate brunch every Saturday in your Fellowship Hall. Your structure was eye-opening. I saw dedicated church members, community volunteers, and homeless people, referred to as "guests" working almost seamlessly to pull off a weekly brunch and clothing pantry. I too availed myself of your extraordinary hospitality while on the streets and even had a favorite sleeping spot in the lot. Here, I met old and new friends, and struggled side-by-side as we faced the demands of the weather, the noise, and night sirens on the streets, and the always potential unknown dangers. I washed feet on Holy Thursday in the alley behind your church and sometimes dropped in to volunteer at brunch time.

St. Ignatius Martyr Catholic Church, thank you for hosting *Freeze Night* on Sunday nights November – March. When the temperature dips to 32 degrees or 35 and rainy, you open your doors to 100 homeless men who are delivered to the school gym by city busses for an evening meal and a night of safety, warmth, and welcome. I have been honored to sleep with these guests since 2008.

In 2010, The Roman Catholic Diocese of Austin required all deaconate candidates who were in the final stages of their study and discernment to spend a weekend learning about the homeless population in Austin. Alan Graham led a group of men who we called the country mice, as they stayed in the woods. I led a group of men we called the city mice who hid out in the city with me. Jimmy, a homeless friend, and I sandwiched our ten lambs between us at night to keep them safe. Thank you Catholic Diocese leadership for remembering that our city and parishes are full of many kinds of people, all of us in need of love and mercy. The Roman Catholic Diocese of Austin includes 123 parishes and missions, six university Catholic student centers in 25 counties in Central Texas.

Thank you Caritas of Austin, a nonprofit organization, for being there, working with the homeless population including providing a hot meal at noon each weekday and for feeding me and treating me with dignity while I was on the streets. The same goes for Trinity Center, of Austin, an outgrowth of concern from parishioners of St. David's Episcopal Church that cares for homeless people in the downtown area. I was introduced to you by a homeless friend. You too treated me with extraordinary kindness when I attended a Monday *Woman to Woman* breakfast, birthday celebration, and clothing pantry morning. For these few hours, while living on the streets, I felt cherished as a woman. You served tea and coffee in china cups, some chipped but still lovely, fresh fruit and tiny muffins, and homemade birthday cake, which surely said, "Someone cares."

All Things Faithful, a faith-driven media company based in Austin, TX, deserves a shout-out. Their mission is "to glorify God in all things by advocating faith into our everyday lives." Founded in 2017, their weekly posts include reflections, spotlights on persons of faith, resources for programs, study, music, and merchandise. I have been a guest writer for a number of their posts. Their attractive and innovate faith-based approach to social media has created a growing fan base.

Finally, a big hurrah and kudos to the *Austin American-Statesman* newspaper. When I moved to Austin in 2000 from the east coast, I could not believe that every Saturday, there was a Faith section in a city paper called, "In Your Words," representing people from all faiths. Since 2008, I am proud to be a contributing writer. Other pieces that I have written have appeared in the Statesman in guest's columns, or in features such as "Around the City" or "Others Say." Informed citizens, with news and articles touching every arena of their lives, make cities cohesive and robust. Thank you Statesman for bringing us together!

ABOUT THE AUTHOR

Judith Knotts is a failed violinist and tap dancer. Her professional career has centered on education as a consultant to schools, school head, and writer. She is interested in how human beings develop and become who they are. Dr. Knotts' journey into the homeless world began when she was in her sixties and continues into her seventies. She believes change always brings with it an invitation to become our best selves.

ABOUT THE COVER ARTIST

Laura Tanier was my friend who also happened to be homeless. I met her in May of 2003 on the first full day of a 72-hour-plus retreat, where I was with a group of people living on the streets with no money, no credit card, and no cell phone.

The first night of the retreat, I slept in an alley, closed in by an iron gate that in truth was more psychologically comforting than secure. Others slept in a "safe house," while a small band of brave men took to the streets and slept God knows where. The next day, I said to those risk-takers, "I want to go with you tonight." They mumbled half-heartedly, "Okay," wondering what in the world to do with a sixty-something-year-old woman while they went "dumpster-diving" with their newly found homeless friends.

Taking all of this in, Laura, who was sitting nearby in the park, said, "Come stay with me, you don't want to go with them." When I asked, "Why," and imagined her response—"You will be assaulted or raped"—she stunned me by saying, "They use bad language." Now Laura and I were nearly strangers. She did not know that I was a grandmother and head of a school, but somehow she zeroed in on who I was and felt I would be offended by the roughness.

I spent the next two nights sleeping outside next to a first floor porch of an abandoned building. Laura's secret home was the second floor porch. She explained her gifts to me—a piece of cardboard that would make a mattress and an empty peanut butter jar, a daunting substitute for a toilet. I used the cardboard gratefully, but not the jar. These treasures were the first of many gifts from my new friend. I trusted Laura enough to go with her to a spot I knew not where, in a city where I was a relative stranger and it worked out fine.

In turn, Laura trusted me the next day by presenting me with hundreds of handwritten pages, a draft of her first book. She wanted me to read it and give her feedback. I asked if it was her only copy and she said "Yes." Hearing this, I felt that I just could not take it. What if something happened while I was carrying it or sleeping with it near me? Laura was confident in her book's safekeeping and insisted that I hold on to it. Generously sharing her soul and her street-smarts with a stranger made us fast friends until her death.

Laura was unique. She grew up with extended family in a crowded Hogan on an Indian reservation. Her mother was Native American, her dad English. She told me as a child that she was a shepherdess who tended the families' sheep throughout the reservation. Early on, she and those around her must have recognized her many differences. Exceedingly smart and creative in math, science, and the arts, she was not like other children or young people. In addition, Laura believed she was a woman in a man's body. She left the reservation, her people, hoping that she would learn more about technology and come back to teach them. This did not happen.

While living on the streets, Laura wrote an extensive autobiography, and most of a draft of a historical fiction novel set in the ice age. She earned a degree in engineering from The University of Texas, and was most proud of receiving a grant from the National Endowment of the Arts. With this grant, Laura traveled by bus to Dallas for the Writer's Workshop, stayed in a hotel for a week, and interacted with other artists, a rare treat for a woman who normally slept on the streets and stood in line for food handed out in soup kitchens and trucks.

As a transgender homeless woman, Laura could have faced many obstacles. At first glance, she was distinct. Her manly frame and frequent shadow of facial hair was contrasted by blond-grey curls often bobbing under a floppy hat, a flowery dress and a small silver cross at her neck. People, homeless and those with homes, respected her for her authenticity and her quiet grace and generosity. Laura told me, "I cannot give money to organizations, but I am a citizen of the city and can give my time and talent." She was a valued and loyal volunteer to various church and civic organizations.

Laura's life was unusual in most ways. Despite her gifts, like many people, she did not fit into a mold. For a brief time, she worked in a lab on the night shift. And for another short time, she lived in public housing. Neither of these situations worked out. With no hard feelings and amazing resilience, Laura returned to her street life.

Being homeless is stressful to the body and mind. Laura suffered a stroke during the time we were friends and after this she moved slowly. A hit-and-run driver ran a red light and crashed into her while she was crossing a street.

I had missed seeing Laura for weeks and had no way to contact her. I walked the streets and talked to everyone I knew to find out where she was. A homeless friend told me what had happened and where I could find Laura. I went to the hospital immediately. I had to gown myself from head to toe so I would not bring any germs into her room. She was very vulnerable to infection. It was Holy week—March 2008. I brought Laura a little Easter basket that made her smile. We visited briefly as she was very weak. I told her I loved her and left, not realizing that this was the final goodbye. She died of her injuries a short time later.

Laura's painting, 22 x 28 inches acrylic, which is used as the cover of *You Are My Brother*, hangs in my home. I bought it at an Arts Fair for Homeless Artists years ago. It shouts of her multifaceted brilliance and her belief that every one of us is colorfully unique—connected to each other in startling ways.

A NOTE FROM THE AUTHOR

Thank you for purchasing *You Are My Brother*. Although it's a collection of stories, at its core, it is an inspirational book meant to connect all of us to a distinctly different environment and to each other—stimulating reflection and possibly change.

I hope you enjoyed reading it! If you did, please share the book and your thoughts about it with family, friends, colleagues, classmates, neighbors, and groups to which you belong. For me, recommending a book, or better yet giving a book, is a peek into the person I am inside. I often wonder, who am I really? And who are you—my child, my friend, my partner? Exchanging stories, ideas, and books is a good place to begin our search for meaning and belonging.

After reading, *You Are My Brother*, why not start a lively conversation about some of the stories in the collection such as *Holy Families* or

Dignity or *Being Loved* and see where it takes you. It doesn't have to be a formal book group discussion. Today, we chat about all sorts of issues that interest us and tackle situations that bother us in emails and in social media with strangers and with people we know. The connecting just feels good and it's so easy.

Let's talk as well! I want to know—what resonated with you in the book? What concerned you? What stuck with you? What changed you in any way? And, tell me how my experiences with a homeless person and a homeless community were like or unlike yours?

Then, ask yourself if you feel the slightest nudge to move on to the next step, whatever it may be, to enrich your life and extend a hand to our homeless brothers and sisters.

I'm behind you all the way!

Contact me at: YouAreMyBrotherBook@gmail.com

INDEX

A

B

Made in the USA
Coppell, TX
15 March 2021